PLANNING GUIDE

Houghton
Mifflin
Harcourt

2016 Edition

Copyright © by Houghton Mifflin Harcourt Publishing Company

Printed in the U.S.A.

ISBN 978-0-544-71207-2

2 3 4 5 6 7 8 9 10 0607   24 23 22 21 20 19 18 17 16 15
4500570936   ^ B C D E F G

Table of Contents

PROGRAM OVERVIEW

About *Go Math!*

Program Overview PG4

Digital Resources PG12

Assessment, Diagnosis, Intervention PG14

Authors, Consultants, Reviewers, and Field Test Teachers PG16

Go Math! and the Principles of Effective Mathematics Programs PG18

Math Processes and Practices PG20

Supporting Math Processes and Practices Through Questioning Strategies. . PG23

Math Processes and Practices in *Go Math!* PG24

Planning Resources

Year-At-A-Glance PG30

End-of-Year Planner PG40

END-OF-YEAR RESOURCES

Review Projects

Review Project: Books for Sale PG42

Review Project: Plan a Trip to the Zoo PG44

Review Project: Measuring Up! PG46

Review Project: Shape Designs PG48

Getting Ready for Grade 3

These lessons review prerequisite skills and prepare for next year's content.

Lesson 1: Find Sums on an Addition Table PG50

Lesson 2: Estimate Sums: 2-Digit Addition PG52

Lesson 3: Estimate Sums: 3-Digit Addition PG54

Lesson 4: Estimate Differences: 2-Digit Subtraction PG56

Lesson 5: Estimate Differences: 3-Digit Subtraction PG58

Lesson 6: Order 3-Digit Numbers PG60

Lesson 7: Equal Groups of 2 . . . . .PG62

Lesson 8: Equal Groups of 5 . . . . .PG64

Lesson 9: Equal Groups of 10 . . . . .PG66

Lesson 10: Hands On: Size of Shares PG68

Lesson 11: Hands On: Number of Equal Shares PG70

Lesson 12: Solve Problems with Equal Shares PG72

Getting Ready Test: Lessons 1–12 . . . . .PG74

Lesson 13: Hour Before and Hour After PG76

Lesson 14: Elapsed Time in Hours PG78

Lesson 15: Elapsed Time in Minutes PG80

Lesson 16: Hands On: Capacity • Nonstandard Units PG82

Lesson 17: Describe Measurement Data PG84

Lesson 18: Fraction Models: Thirds and Sixths PG86

Lesson 19: Fraction Models: Fourths and Eighths .PG88

Lesson 20: Compare Fraction Models PG90

Getting Ready Test: Lessons 13–20 . . . . .PG92

Correlations

Grab-and-Go!™ Differentiated Centers Kit PG94

***Go Math!* Sequence Options** PG98

Student Edition Glossary PG100

Professional Development References PG104

Index PG106

It's Effective and Accessible Math

GO Math! for Kindergarten–Grade 6 combines powerful teaching strategies with never-before-seen components, to offer everything needed to successfully build a strong foundation in elementary math skills and concepts.

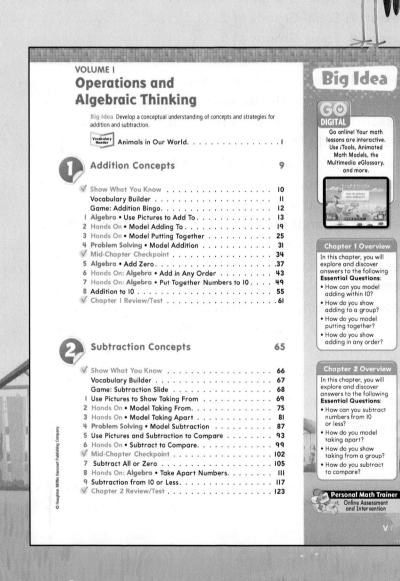

VOLUME 1

Operations and Algebraic Thinking

Big Idea Develop a conceptual understanding of concepts and strategies for addition and subtraction.

Vocabulary Reader Animals in Our World. 1

1 Addition Concepts 9

Show What You Know 10
Vocabulary Builder 11
Game: Addition Bingo. 12
1 Algebra • Use Pictures to Add To 13
2 Hands On • Model Adding To 19
3 Hands On • Model Putting Together 25
4 Problem Solving • Model Addition 31
Mid-Chapter Checkpoint 34
5 Algebra • Add Zero. 37
6 Hands On: Algebra • Add in Any Order 43
7 Hands On: Algebra • Put Together Numbers to 10 49
8 Addition to 10 55
Chapter 1 Review/Test 61

2 Subtraction Concepts 65

Show What You Know 66
Vocabulary Builder 67
Game: Subtraction Slide 68
1 Use Pictures to Show Taking From 69
2 Hands On • Model Taking From. 75
3 Hands On • Model Taking Apart 81
4 Problem Solving • Model Subtraction 87
5 Use Pictures and Subtraction to Compare 93
6 Hands On • Subtract to Compare. 99
Mid-Chapter Checkpoint 102
7 Subtract All or Zero 105
8 Hands On: Algebra • Take Apart Numbers. 111
9 Subtraction from 10 or Less. 117
Chapter 2 Review/Test 123

Big Idea

GO DIGITAL

Go online! Your math lessons are interactive. Use iTools, Animated Math Models, the Multimedia eGlossary, and more.

Chapter 1 Overview

In this chapter, you will explore and discover answers to the following **Essential Questions**:
- How can you model adding within 10?
- How do you show adding to a group?
- How do you model putting together?
- How do you show adding in any order?

Chapter 2 Overview

In this chapter, you will explore and discover answers to the following **Essential Questions**:
- How can you subtract numbers from 10 or less?
- How do you model taking apart?
- How do you show taking from a group?
- How do you subtract to compare?

Personal Math Trainer
Online Assessment and Intervention

© Houghton Mifflin Harcourt Publishing Company

perfect for
21st century students.

GO Math! gets students engaged with learning, focused on working smarter, and ready for the future. The Interactive Student Edition offers the unique Personal Math Trainer® Powered by Knewton™—a state of the art online, and adaptive, assessment, and intervention system. In this tablet-based, mobile, and online environment, students receive a completely personalized learning experience, focused on in-depth understanding, fluency, and application of standards.

A way of thinking about learning,

GO Math! helps students engage with content and the mathematical processes in new ways. Lessons begin with problem-based situations and then build to more abstract problems. All along the way, students use multiple models, manipulatives, quick pictures, and symbols to build mathematical understandings. And, best of all, **GO Math!** is write-in at every grade level, so students are completely engaged.

GO Math! practice, homework, and review pages are included in the Student Edition!

that truly prepares students for High-Stakes Assessments.

GO Math! works! Using manipulatives, multiple models, and rich, rigorous questions, students move through a carefully sequenced arc of learning where they develop deep conceptual understanding, and then practice, apply, and discuss what they know with skill and confidence.

An online teacher tool offering the functionality of a planner...

GO Math! helps with the big jobs of teaching. Using the Teacher Dashboard and Smart Planner, teachers create lesson plans and access great resources that can be sequenced to align with district requirements or classroom needs. There's more. The **GO Math!** technology and classroom instruction work together. Students alternate often between engaging with their teacher and classmates and focusing on online content personalized to their learning pace and progress.

Math on the Spot videos, available for every lesson in _GO Math!_, support teachers and students, within the classroom and at home.

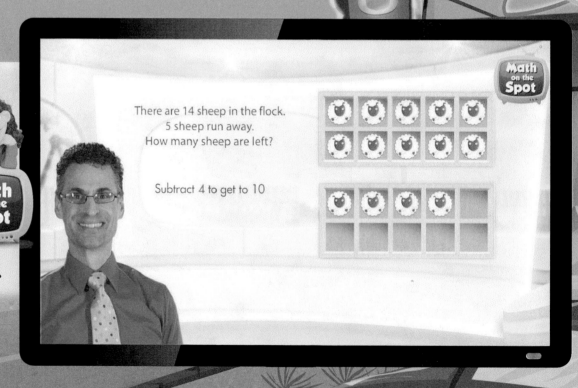

There are 14 sheep in the flock.
5 sheep run away.
How many sheep are left?

Subtract 4 to get to 10

with the convenience of mobile.

Access to all of these great resources is right at your finger tips, saving you valuable planning and teaching time.

Create daily lesson plans with a single search.

Organize resources quickly.

See a snapshot of recent student report data.

Grab-and-Go Resources,

GO Math! works for the busy teacher. Everything from Teacher Editions to activity centers to manipulatives are organized in a ready-made, grab-and-go way to save you time.

GO Math! Teacher Editions are color-coded by Big Idea and organized by chapters to help teachers quickly identify materials and flexibly organize their curriculum. And instruction is organized around the 5 Es—Engage, Explore, Explain, Elaborate, and Evaluate. With this approach, **GO Math!** emphasizes in-depth understanding and communication within an engaging, inclusive classroom environment.

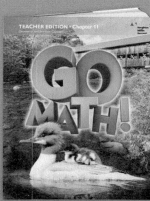

perfect for the busy teacher.

The *Grab-and-Go!™ Differentiated Centers Kits* are ready-made, differentiated math centers with activities, games, and literature. Resources for every lesson and special challenge materials make the *Grab-and-Go!™ Differentiated Centers Kits* the perfect resource for independent practice.

Digital Resources

FOR LEARNING...

 Interactive Student Edition

- Immerses students in an interactive, multi-sensory math environment
- Enhances learning with scaffolded, interactive instruction and just-in-time feedback
- Provides audio reinforcement for each lesson
- Makes learning a two-way experience, using a variety of interactive tools

FOR ASSESSMENT AND INTERVENTION...

 Personal Math Trainer

- Creates a personalized learning path for each student
- Provides opportunities for practice, homework, and assessment
- Includes worked-out examples and helpful video support
- Offers targeted intervention and extra support to build proficiency and understanding

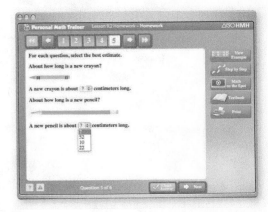

FOR DAILY MATH TUTORING...

 Math on the Spot Videos

- Models good problem-solving thinking in every lesson
- Engages students through interesting animations and fun characters
- Builds student problem-solving proficiency and confidence
- Builds the skills needed for success on high-stakes assessments

FOR TEACHING...

Interactive Teacher Digital Management Center

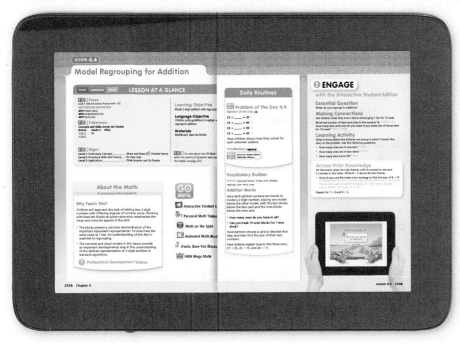

Teacher Edition

- Plan your lessons from the convenience of your classroom, at home, or on the go
- View student lessons 24/7
- Access *Math on the Spot* videos anytime, anywhere
- Offers learning and instructional activities and suggestions

Professional Development Videos

- Learn more about the content
- See first-hand the integration of the Math Processes and Practices
- Watch students engaged in a productive struggle

DIGITAL RESOURCE...

Digital Management System

- Manage online all program content and components
- Search for and select resources
- Identify resources based on student ability and needs
- View and assign student lessons, practice, assessments, and more

Assessment ➡ Diagnosis ➡ Intervention

Data-Driven Decision Making

Go Math! allows for quick and accurate data-driven decision making so you can spend more instructional time tailored to children's needs.

Program Assessment Options with Intervention

Diagnostic

To allow children to be engaged from the beginning of the year

- **Prerequisite Skills Inventory** in *Chapter Resources*
- **Beginning-of-Year Test** in *Chapter Resources*
- **Show What You Know** in *Student Edition*

- **Intensive Intervention**
- **Intensive Intervention User Guide**
- **Strategic Intervention**
- **Personal Math Trainer**

Formative

To monitor children's understanding of lessons and to adjust instruction accordingly

- **Lesson Quick Check** in *Teacher Edition*
- **Lesson Practice** in *Student Edition*
- **Mid-Chapter Checkpoint** in *Student Edition*
- **Portfolio** in *Chapter Resources and Teacher Edition*
- **Middle-of-Year Test** in *Chapter Resources*

- **Reteach** with each lesson
- **RtI: Tier 1 and Tier 2 Activities** online
- **Personal Math Trainer**

Summative

To determine whether children have achieved the chapter objectives

- **Chapter Review/Test** in *Student Edition*
- **Chapter Test** in *Chapter Resources* (high-stakes assessment formats)
- **Performance Assessment Task** in *Chapter Resources*
- **End-of-Year Test** in *Chapter Resources*
- **Getting Ready for Grade 3 Test** in *Getting Ready Lessons and Resources*

- **Reteach** with each lesson
- **RtI: Tier 1 and Tier 2 Activities** online
- **Personal Math Trainer**

© Houghton Mifflin Harcourt Publishing Company • Image Credits: (bg) ©Krys Bailey/Alamy

Tracking Yearly Progress

Beginning of the Year

The Beginning-of-Year Test determines how many of this year's important concepts children already understand. Adjust lesson pacing for skills that need light coverage and allow more time for skills children find challenging.

During the Year

Chapter Tests, Performance Tasks, and the Middle-of-Year Test monitor children's progress throughout the year. Plan time to reinforce skills children have not mastered.

End of the Year

The End-of-Year Test assesses children's mastery of this year's important concepts. Reinforce skills that children find challenging in order to provide the greatest possible success.

Performance Assessment

Performance Assessment helps to reveal the thinking strategies children use to solve problems. The Performance Tasks, in *GO Math!* can be used to complete the picture for how children reason about mathematics.

GO Math! has a Performance Task for each Chapter and each Big Idea. Each assessment has several tasks that target specific math concepts, skills, and strategies. These tasks can help assess children's ability to use what they have learned to solve everyday problems. Teachers can plan for children to complete one task at a time or use an extended amount of time to complete the entire assessment. Projects for each Big Idea also serve to assess children's problem solving strategies and understanding of mathematical concepts they learn in the Big Idea.

The Performance Tasks and Big Idea Projects offer the following features:

- They model good instruction.
- They are diagnostic.
- They encourage the thinking process.
- They are flexible.
- They use authentic instruction.
- They are scored holistically.

GO Math! also has optional Diagnostic Interview Assessment at the beginning of each chapter to help determine each child's readiness for the content in the chapter. The Diagnostic Interview assesses children at the concrete or pictorial level. Intervention options are provided.

 ## *GO Math!* Personal Math Trainer

- HTML5-based online homework, assessment, and intervention engine
- Pre-built online homework, tests, and intervention (with Personal Study Plans)
- Algorithmic, tech-enhanced items, with wrong answer feedback, and learning aids

Authors

Edward B. Burger, Ph.D.
President, Southwestern University
Georgetown, Texas

Juli K. Dixon, Ph.D.
Professor, Mathematics Education
University of Central Florida
Orlando, Florida

Matthew R. Larson, Ph.D.
K-12 Curriculum Specialist for Mathematics
Lincoln Public Schools
Lincoln, Nebraska

Martha E. Sandoval-Martinez
Math Instructor
El Camino College
Torrance, California

Steven J. Leinwand
Principal Research Analyst
American Institutes for Research (AIR)
Washington, D.C.

Contributor and Consultant

Rena Petrello
Professor, Mathematics
Moorpark College
Moorpark, CA

Elizabeth Jiménez
CEO, GEMAS Consulting
Professional Expert on English Learner Education
Bilingual Education and Dual Language
Pomona, California

© Houghton Mifflin Harcourt Publishing Company • Image Credits: (bg) ©Krys Bailey/Alamy

Go Math! Reviewers and Field Test Teachers

Janine L. Ambrose
Instructional Coach
Grades Taught: K–7
Sunset Ridge Elementary
Pendergast Elementary School District
Phoenix, Arizona

Patricia R. Barbour
Teacher: Grade 2
Sara Lindemuth Primary School
Susquehanna Township School District
Harrisburg, Pennsylvania

Pamela Bauer
Speech/Language Pathologist, M.A., CCC/SLP
Special School District of St. Louis County
Kindergarten Interventionist
Arrowpoint Elementary
Hazelwood, Missouri

James Brohn
Principal
Morning Star Lutheran School
Jackson, Wisconsin

Earl S. Brown
Teacher: Middle School Math
Susquehanna Township Middle School
Susquehanna Township School District
Harrisburg, Pennsylvania

Rebecca Centerino
Teacher: Grade 1
Zitzman Elementary
Meramec Valley RIII School District
Pacific, Missouri

Jessica Z. Jacobs
Assistant Principal
Thomas Holtzman Junior Elementary School
Susquehanna Township School District
Harrisburg, Pennsylvania

Tonya Leonard
Teacher: Grade 3
Peine Ridge Elementary
Wentzville RIV School District
Wentzville, Missouri

Jennifer Love Frier
Teacher: Grade 1
Olathe School District
Olathe, Kansas

Michelle Mieger
Teacher: Grade 3
Cedar Springs Elementary
Northwest R-1
House Springs, Missouri

Jeanne K. Selissen
Teacher: Grade 4
Tewksbury School District
Tewksbury, Massachusetts

Jo Ellen Showers
Teacher: Grade K
Sara Lindemuth Primary School
Susquehanna Township School District
Harrisburg, Pennsylvania

Judith M. Stagoski
Grades Taught: 5–8
District: Archdiocese of St. Louis
St. Louis, Missouri

Pauline Von Hoffer
Grades Taught: 4–12
Curriculum Coordinator
Wentzville School District
Wentzville, Missouri

Go Math! and the Principles of Effective Mathematics Programs

PROFESSIONAL DEVELOPMENT

by Matthew R. Larson, Ph.D.
K-12 Curriculum Specialist for Mathematics
Lincoln Public Schools
Lincoln, Nebraska

All education researchers strongly agree that two components of effective mathematics programs have a positive impact on student learning: the implemented curriculum and teachers' implementation of research-informed instructional practices.

Go Math! uniquely provides both elements: a strong curriculum aligned to current expectations, and a design that robustly supports teachers' research-informed instructional practices.

The Curriculum

The power of the curriculum to affect how much students learn in mathematics is well established (Marzano, 2003; Schmoker, 2011). The National Council of Teachers of Mathematics (2014, p. 70) has argued that "an excellent mathematics program includes curriculum that develops important mathematics along coherent learning progressions."

That is precisely how we designed *Go Math!* Its scope and sequence are designed in accord with the latest research on learning progressions (Clements and Sarama, 2014). The curriculum makes connections between and among various mathematical topics, and it is coherent, rigorous, and focused.

The favorable outcome is that students learn each grade level's important mathematics at a deep level while simultaneously connecting each lesson to the bigger ideas of mathematics. In *Go Math!* an optimal proportion of the tasks students work on to develop their understanding as well as their proficiency require complex thought and reasoning – the tasks are not merely harder.

Research-Informed Instructional Practices

A coherent and rigorous curriculum is one of two critical components of a mathematics program that helps ensure the success of all students. The second critical component is an instructional approach based on research-informed instructional practices. The overarching message in NCTM's publication *Principles to Actions: Ensuring Mathematical Success for All* is that "effective teaching is the nonnegotiable core that ensures all students learn mathematics at high levels" (NCTM, 2014, p. 4). NCTM offers eight research-informed instructional strategies to support effective teaching and learning of mathematics. *Go Math!* embeds those eight instructional strategies in the curriculum. These strategies are shown in the table on page PG19.

Embedded Professional Development Support

As authors we appreciate that you are being asked to teach more mathematics at deeper levels than ever before. Teaching mathematics effectively is a complex endeavor, and it takes time to integrate new instructional strategies into your practice. Toward that end *Go Math!* embeds professional development resources into the curriculum. In a series of professional development videos, *Go Math!* coauthor Juli Dixon models successful teaching practices and strategies in real classrooms. These videos are an invaluable resource as you work collaboratively with your colleagues to ensure that all students successfully attain the standards and that you grow in your own knowledge of mathematics and highly effective instructional strategies.

Instructional Strategies...	In *Go Math!*...
1 Establish mathematics goals to focus learning. Effective teaching establishes clear goals, situates goals within learning progressions, and uses the goals to guide instructional decisions (NCTM, 2014, p. 12).	*The goals are clearly labeled in Go Math! More importantly, the scope and sequence have been built around learning progressions and the big ideas of mathematics.*
2 Implement tasks that promote reasoning and problem solving. Effective teaching engages students in solving and discussing tasks that promote mathematical reasoning and problem solving and allow multiple entry points and varied solution strategies (NCTM, 2014, p. 17).	*The 5E lesson framework in Go Math! helps ensure that students explore worthwhile mathematical tasks in every lesson to develop their understanding.*
3 Use and connect mathematical representations. Effective teaching engages students in making connections to deepen understanding of concepts and procedures and as tools for problem solving (NCTM, 2014, p. 24).	*Students move systematically from concrete representations, to their own drawn representations on their MathBoards, and finally to symbolic mathematics.*
4 Facilitate meaningful mathematical discourse. Effective teaching facilitates discourse among students to build shared understanding by analyzing and comparing student approaches and arguments (NCTM, 2014, p. 29).	*Math Talk is a central feature of Go Math! Question prompts and sample dialogue in the Teacher Edition support you as you engage students to develop their conceptual understanding.*
5 Pose purposeful questions. Effective teaching uses purposeful questions to assess and advance students' reasoning and sense making (NCTM, 2014, p. 35).	*The Teacher Edition has many question prompts you can use to generate mathematical discourse, determine what students currently know, and advance their learning. These prompts allow you to transform your classroom into an interactive, student-centered learning environment.*
6 Build procedural fluency from conceptual understanding. Effective teaching builds fluency with procedures so that students become skillful in using procedures flexibly as they solve contextual and mathematical problems (NCTM, 2014, p. 42).	*The goal in Go Math! is for students to learn efficient methods for solving procedures based on understanding. Student learning of traditional algorithms starts with concrete models connected to underlying concepts. Eventually students draw their own representations and finally work with efficient algorithms so their proficiency prepares them to learn future mathematics.*
7 Support productive struggle in learning mathematics. Effective teaching consistently provides students with opportunities and supports to engage in productive struggle as they grapple with mathematical ideas and relationships (NCTM, 2014, p. 48).	*The 5E lesson framework supports students' continued engagement with mathematical concepts. Students have ample time to explore concepts prior to the explain phase of the lesson and are supported with significant guided practice as part of the elaborate phase.*
8 Elicit and use evidence of student thinking. Effective teaching uses evidence of student thinking to assess progress and to adjust instruction continually in ways that support and extend learning (NCTM, 2014, p. 53).	*The question prompts as well as Show What You Know in each chapter, Share and Show with Quick Check in each lesson, Mid-Chapter Checkpoints, and Summative Assessment options at the end of each chapter provide teachers continual and real-time options to use evidence of student thinking to adjust and guide instruction. These diagnostic assessments provide teachers differentiated instructional materials to support all students.*

Math Processes and Practices

Developing Processes and Proficiencies in Mathematics Learners

PROFESSIONAL DEVELOPMENT

by Juli K. Dixon, Ph.D.
Professor, Mathematics Education
University of Central Florida
Orlando, Florida

According to *Principles to Actions* (National Council of Teachers of Mathematics, 2014), "An excellent mathematics program requires effective teaching that engages students in meaningful learning through individual and collaborative experiences that promote their ability to make sense of mathematical ideas and reason mathematically" (p. 5). What this means for elementary school students and how to engage students in this sort of meaningful learning is addressed in the following article.

There are eight Mathematical Processes and Practices. They are based on the National Council of Teachers of Mathematics' (NCTM) *Process Standards* (NCTM, 2000) and the National Research Council's (NRC) *Strands of Mathematical Proficiency* (NRC, 2001). Students who are engaged in the mathematical processes and practices around important mathematics are likely engaged in meaningful learning as described in *Principles to Actions.*

It is likely that good teachers can find evidence of each of these standards for mathematical practice in their current teaching. Regardless, it is useful to examine them and think about how each contributes to the development of mathematically proficient students. What follows is a description of how they might look in an elementary school classroom. Each of these examples is reflective of experiences supported by *Go Math!*

Go Math! supports the Math Processes and Practices through several specific features including:

- Lessons focused on depth of content knowledge,

- Unlock the Problem sections to begin lessons,

- Math Talk questions prompting students to use varied strategies and to explain their reasoning,

- Support for manipulative use and drawings directly on the student pages,

- Prompts that lead students to write their own problems or to determine if the reasoning of others is reasonable, and

- Real-world problems that encourage students to develop productive dispositions.

MPPI: Problem Solving

This process brings to mind developing a productive disposition as described in *Adding It Up* (NRC, 2001). In order for students to develop the diligence intended with this process, they must be provided with problems for which a pathway toward a solution is not immediately evident. If students are asked to determine how much of a cookie each person would receive if 4 cookies were shared among 5 people, a solution pathway is evident if students understand fractions. The students could simply divide each cookie into five equal pieces and give each person one fifth of each cookie or $\frac{4}{5}$ of a cookie in all. Now, consider the same problem given the constraint that the first three cookies are each broken into two equal pieces to start and each person is given half of a cookie.

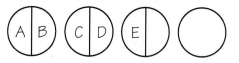

The problem is now more interesting and challenging. How will the remaining pieces of cookies be distributed among the five people? How will the students determine how much of a cookie each person has in all when all the cookies are shared? The students will likely refer back to the context of the problem to make sense of how to solve it. They will also very likely use pictures in their solution process. A solution is within reach, but it will require diligence to persevere in reaching it.

MPP2: Abstract and Quantitative Reasoning

Story problems provide important opportunities for young learners to make sense of mathematics around them. Students often use strategies including acting out the problem to make sense of a solution path. Another important strategy is for students to make sense of the problem situation by determining a number sentence that could represent the problem and then solving it in a mathematically proficient way. Consider the following problem: *Jessica has 7 key chains in her collection. How many more does she need to have 15 key chains all together?*

A student is presented with this problem, but rather than focusing on key words, the student uses the story to make sense of a solution process. The student knows to start with 7 then add something to that to get 15. The student represents this story abstractly by writing $7 + \_\_\_ = 15$. Then the student reasons quantitatively by thinking $7 + 3 = 10$ and $10 + 5 = 15$, so $7 + 8$ must equal 15 (because 3 and 5 are 8). The student then returns to the problem to see if a solution of 8 key chains makes sense. In doing so, the student makes "sense of quantities and their relationships in problem situations" (NGA Center/CCSSO, 2010, p. 6).

MPP3: Use and Evaluate Logical Reasoning

Students need to explain and justify their solution strategies. They should also listen to the explanations of other students and try to make sense of them. They will then be able to incorporate the reasoning of others into their own strategies and improve upon their own solutions. An example of this follows.

A group of students explores formulas for areas of quadrilaterals. Students make sense of the formula for the area of a parallelogram as $b \times h$ by decomposing parallelograms and composing a rectangle with the same area. Following this exploration, a student conjectures that the formula for the area of the trapezoid is also $b \times h$. The student draws this picture and says that the trapezoid can be "turned into" a rectangle with the same base by "moving one triangle over to the other side."

This student has constructed a viable argument based on a special type of trapezoid. Another student agrees that this formula works for an isosceles trapezoid but asks if it will also work for a general trapezoid. This

second student has made sense of the reasoning of the first student and asked a question to help improve the argument.

MPP4: Mathematical Modeling

Students need opportunities to use mathematics to solve real-world problems. As students learn more mathematics, the ways they model situations with mathematics should become more efficient. Consider the problem: *Riley has 4 blue erasers, Alex has 4 yellow erasers, and Paige has 4 purple erasers. How many erasers do they have in all?* A young student would likely model this problem with $4 + 4 + 4$. However, a mathematically proficient student in third grade should model the same situation with 3×4. This demonstrates how modeling will evolve through a student's experiences in mathematics and will change as his or her understanding grows.

A useful strategy for making sense of mathematics is for students to develop real-life contexts to correspond to mathematical expressions. This supports the reflexive relationship that if a student can write a word problem for a given expression, then the student can model a similar word problem with mathematics. Consider $\frac{4}{5} - \frac{1}{2}$. If a student is able to create a word problem to support this fraction subtraction, then, given a word problem, the student is more likely to be able to model the word problem with mathematics and solve it.

MPP5: Use Mathematical Tools

At first glance, one might think that this practice refers to technological tools exclusively, however, tools also include paper and pencil, number lines, and manipulatives (or concrete models). Mathematically proficient students are able to determine which tool to use for a given task. An example to illustrate this practice involves multiplying fractions. A student might choose to use a number line for one problem and paper and pencil procedures for another. If presented the problem $\frac{1}{3} \times \frac{3}{4}$, a mathematically proficient student might draw a number line and divide the distance from 0 to 1 into 4 equal parts drawing a darker line through the first three fourths. That student would see that $\frac{1}{3}$ of the $\frac{3}{4}$ is $\frac{1}{4}$ of the whole.

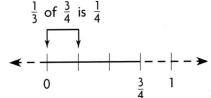

$\frac{1}{3}$ of $\frac{3}{4}$ is $\frac{1}{4}$

However, the same student presented with the problem $\frac{1}{3} \times \frac{4}{7}$ might not use a drawing at all, but might find it more efficient to multiply the numerators and the denominators of the factors to get $\frac{4}{21}$ as the product. Both solution paths illustrate strategic use of tools for the given problems.

MPP6: Use Precise Mathematical Language

An important aspect of precision in mathematics is developed through the language used to describe it. This can be illustrated with definitions of geometric shapes. A kindergarten student is not expected to classify quadrilaterals. However, it is appropriate for a kindergarten student to name and describe shapes including squares and rectangles. Teachers seeking to support kindergarten students to attend to precision will include squares within sets of other rectangles so that these students will not use the language that all rectangles have two long sides and two short sides. These same students will be more likely to be able to correctly classify squares and rectangles in third grade because of this attention to precision when they are in kindergarten.

MPP7: See Structure

Students who have made sense of strategies based on properties for finding products of single digit factors (basic facts) will be more likely to apply those properties when exploring multidigit multiplication. Consider the importance of the distributive property in looking for and making use of structure in this case. A student who has made sense of 6×7 by solving 6×5 and 6×2 has used a strategy based on the distributive property where 6×7 can be thought of as $6 \times (5 + 2)$ and then the 6 can be "distributed over" the 5 and 2. This same student can apply the distributive property to make sense of 12×24 by thinking of 24 as $20 + 4$ and solving $12 \times 20 + 12 \times 4$. A student who can make sense of multidigit multiplication in this way is on a good path to making sense of the structure of the standard algorithm for multidigit multiplication.

MPP8: Generalize

Whether performing simple calculations or solving complex problems, students should take advantage of the regularity of mathematics. If students who are exploring the volume of right rectangular prisms are given centimeter cubes and grid paper, they can build a prism with a given base and explore how the volume changes as the height of the prism increases. Students who look for ways to describe the change should see that the height of the prism is a factor of the volume of the prism and that if the area of the base is known, the volume of the prism is determined by multiplying the area of the base by the height of the prism. Identifying this pattern and repeated reasoning will help students build an understanding of the formula for the volume of right rectangular prisms.

As evidenced by the examples of mathematical processes and practices in elementary school classrooms, "a lack of understanding effectively prevents a student from engaging in the mathematical practices" (NGA Center/CCSSO, 2010, p. 8). Teachers address this challenge by focusing on mathematical processes and practices while developing an understanding of the content they support. In so doing, this process facilitates the development of mathematically proficient students.

Supporting Math Processes and Practices Through Questioning

When you ask...	*Students...*
• What is the problem asking? • How will you use that information? • What other information do you need? • Why did you choose that operation? • What is another way to solve that problem? • What did you do first? Why? • What can you do if you don't know how to solve a problem? • Have you solved a problem similar to this one? • When did you realize your first method would not work for this problem? • How do you know your answer makes sense?	Use problem solving.
• What is a situation that could be represented by this equation? • What operation did you use to represent the situation? • Why does that operation represent the situation? • What properties did you use to find the answer? • How do you know your answer is reasonable?	Use abstract and quantitative reasoning.
• Will that method always work? • How do you know? • What do you think about what she said? • Who can tell us about a different method? • What do you think will happen if...? • When would that not be true? • Why do you agree/disagree with what he said? • What do you want to ask her about that method? • How does that drawing support your work?	Use and evaluate logical reasoning.
• Why is that a good model for this problem? • How can you use a simpler problem to help you find the answer? • What conclusions can you make from your model? • How would you change your model if...?	Use mathematical modeling.
• What could you use to help you solve the problem? • What strategy could you use to make that calculation easier? • How would estimation help you solve that problem? • Why did you decide to use...?	Use mathematical tools.
• How do you know your answer is reasonable? • How can you use math vocabulary in your explanation? • How do you know those answers are equivalent? • What does that mean?	Use precise mathematical language.
• How did you discover that pattern? • What other patterns can you find? • What rule did you use to make this group? • Why can you use that property in this problem? • How is that like...?	See structure.
• What do you remember about...? • What happens when...? • What if you...instead of...? • What might be a shortcut for...?	Generalize.

Math Processes and Practices in *Go Math!*

Math Processes and Practices	Throughout *Go Math!* Look for...	Explanation
1. Problem Solving Mathematically proficient students start by explaining to themselves the meaning of a problem and looking for entry points to its solution. They analyze givens, constraints, relationships, and goals. They make conjectures about the form and meaning of the solution and plan a solution pathway, rather than simply jumping into a solution attempt. They consider analogous problems and try special cases and simpler forms of the original problem in order to gain insight into its solution. They monitor and evaluate their progress and change course if necessary. Mathematically proficient students check their answers to problems using a different method, and they continually ask themselves, "Does this make sense?" and "Is my answer reasonable?" They understand the approaches of others to solving complex problems and identify correspondences between different approaches. Mathematically proficient students understand how mathematical ideas interconnect and build on one another to produce a coherent whole.	**Some Examples:** Problem Solving Lessons Grade K, Lesson 1.9 Grade 1, Lesson 8.8 Grade 2, Lesson 1.7 Unlock the Problem Grade K, Lesson 2.4 Grade 1, Lesson 3.12 Grade 2, Lesson 6.6 Try Another Problem Grade K, Lesson 7.6 Grade 1, Lesson 6.8 Grade 2, Lesson 1.7 Share and Show Grade 1, Lesson 7.3 Grade 2, Lesson 10.2 On Your Own Grade K, Lesson 4.5 Grade 1, Lesson 10.6 Grade 2, Lesson 5.8	**Children learn to:** • analyze a problem. • explain what information they need to find to solve the problem. • determine what information they need to use to solve the problem. • develop a plan for solving the problem. • use concrete objects to conceptualize a problem. • draw quick pictures on MathBoards to help solve problems. • evaluate the solution for reasonableness. **Children learn to:** • look at similar problems and apply techniques used in the original problem to gain insight into the solution of a new problem. • draw quick pictures on MathBoards to help solve problems. • evaluate the solution for reasonableness. • persevere in solving a problem, determining what methods and strategies they have learned that they can apply to solve the problem.

Teacher Edition   Student Edition

Math Processes and Practices	Throughout *Go Math!* Look for...	Explanation
2. Abstract and Quantitative Reasoning Mathematically proficient students make sense of quantities and their relationships in problem situations. They bring two complementary abilities to bear on problems involving quantitative relationships: the ability to decontextualize—to abstract a given situation and represent it symbolically and manipulate the representing symbols as if they have a life of their own, without necessarily attending to their referents— and the ability to contextualize, to pause as needed during the manipulation process in order to probe into the referents for the symbols involved. Quantitative reasoning entails habits of creating a coherent representation of the problem at hand; considering the units involved; attending to the meaning of quantities, not just how to compute them; and knowing and flexibly using different properties of operations and objects.	**Some Examples:** Model and Draw Grade K, Lesson 5.6 Grade 1, Lesson 3.7 Grade 2, Lesson 3.7	**Children learn to:** • abstract a real-world situation and represent it symbolically as a number sentence as a way of solving a problem. • put the numbers and symbols in a number sentence back into the context of the real-world situation for the solution.
	Measurement and Geometry Lessons Grade K, Lesson 12.5 Grade 1, Lesson 11.2 Grade 2, Lesson 8.1	**Children learn to:** • focus on the meaning of quantities in measurement and geometry problems. • choose the most appropriate kind of unit to use to solve a problem.
	Lessons on the properties of operations Grade K, Lesson 6.3 Grade 1, Lesson 3.7 Grade 2, Lesson 3.1	**Children learn to use these properties of operations:** • changing the way addends are grouped in an addition problem does not change the sum. • changing the order of the addends in an addition problem does not change the sum.
	Lessons on modeling with manipulatives and drawings Grade K, Lesson 5.1 Grade 1, Lesson 5.6 Grade 2, Lesson 3.9	**Children learn to:** • represent real-world situations with concrete and pictorial models. • use bar models as one way to visualize addition and subtraction problems symbolically.

Teacher Edition   Student Edition

Math Processes and Practices	Throughout *Go Math!* Look for...	Explanation
3. Use and Evaluate Logical Reasoning Mathematically proficient students understand and use stated assumptions, definitions, and previously established results in constructing arguments. They make conjectures and build a logical progression of statements to explore the truth of their conjectures. They analyze situations by breaking them into cases and recognize and use counterexamples. They organize their mathematical thinking, justify their conclusions and communicate them to others, and respond to the arguments of others. They reason inductively about data, making plausible arguments that take into account the context from which the data arose. Mathematically proficient students are also able to compare the effectiveness of two plausible arguments, distinguish correct logic or reasoning from that which is flawed, and—if there is a flaw in an argument—explain what it is. They justify whether a given statement is true always, sometimes, or never. Mathematically proficient students participate and collaborate in a mathematics community. They listen to or read the arguments of others, decide whether they make sense, and ask useful questions to clarify or improve the arguments.	**Some Examples:** Math Talk Grade 1, Lesson 8.1 Grade 2, Lesson 11.1	**Children learn to:** • use mathematical language. • explain mathematical concepts. • defend, justify, or disprove a mathematical conjecture. • use deductive reasoning, definitions, and previously proven conclusions.
	Vocabulary Builder Grade K Grade 1 Grade 2 Developing Math Language Grade K Grade 1 Grade 2 Vocabulary Preview Grade 1 Grade 2	**Children learn to:** • develop, build, and reinforce mathematics vocabulary. • discuss mathematical definitions. • strengthen their abilities to communicate ideas about mathematics.
	Think Smarter Problems Grade K, Lesson 5.5 Grade 1, Lesson 9.1 Grade 2, Lesson 1.3 Go Deeper Grade K, Lesson 5.5 Grade 1, Lesson 10.4 Grade 2, Lesson 4.3	**Children learn to:** • extend their thinking. • discuss their explanations. • give concrete examples to justify their explanations. • explain and describe mathematical understanding.

Teacher Edition   Student Edition

Math Processes and Practices	Throughout *Go Math!* Look for...	Explanation
4. Mathematical Modeling Mathematically proficient students apply the mathematics they know to solve problems arising in everyday life, society, and the workplace using a variety of appropriate strategies. They create and use a variety of representations to solve problems and to organize and communicate mathematical ideas. Mathematically proficient students apply what they know and are comfortable making assumptions and approximations to simplify a complicated situation, realizing that these may need revision later. They are able to identify important quantities in a practical situation and map their relationships using such tools as diagrams, two-way tables, graphs, flowcharts and formulas. They analyze those relationships mathematically to draw conclusions. They routinely interpret their mathematical results in the context of the situation and reflect on whether the results make sense, possibly improving the model if it has not served its purpose.	**Some Examples:** Unlock the Problem • Real World Grade K, Lesson 6.3 Grade 1, Lesson 7.4 Grade 2, Lesson 8.5	**Children learn to:** • apply the mathematics they know to solve real-world problems. • write a number sentence to describe a situation. • use diagrams, tables, and graphs to help them see relationships and draw conclusions in problems.
	Hands On Lessons Grade K, Lesson 6.4 Grade 1, Lesson 2.8 Grade 2, Lesson 7.4	**Children learn to:** • model in a 'hands-on' approach to analyze problems.
	Connect To... Cross-Curricular Grade K Grade 1 Grade 2 **Literature** Grade K Grade 1 Grade 2	**Children learn to:** • apply the mathematics they know to solve problems in Literature, Science, Social Studies, Art, and other disciplines. • appreciate how mathematics influences their lives in ways both large and small.

Teacher Edition   Student Edition

Math Processes and Practices	Throughout Go Math! Look for...	Explanation
5. Use Mathematical Tools Mathematically proficient students consider the available tools when solving a mathematical problem. These tools might include pencil and paper, models, a ruler, a protractor, a calculator, a spreadsheet, a computer algebra system, a statistical package, or dynamic geometry software. Mathematically proficient students are sufficiently familiar with tools appropriate for their grade or course to make sound decisions about when each of these tools might be helpful, recognizing both the insight to be gained and their limitations. Mathematically proficient students identify relevant external mathematical resources, such as digital content, and use them to pose or solve problems. They use technological tools to explore and deepen their understanding of concepts and to support the development of learning mathematics. They use technology to contribute to concept development, simulation, representation, reasoning, communication and problem solving.	**Some Examples:** Hands-On Lessons Grade K, Lesson 3.1 Grade 1, Lesson 12.3 Grade 2, Lesson 8.1	**Children learn to:** • use available tools to analyze problems through a concrete 'hands-on' approach.
	Geometry and Measurement Lessons Grade K, Lesson 11.4 Grade 1, Lesson 9.4 Grade 2, Lesson 8.8	**Children learn to use appropriate tools to:** • enhance and deepen their understanding of measurement and geometry concepts.
	Digital Path iTools Animated Math Models HMH Mega Math All student lessons	**Children learn to use technological tools to:** • enhance and deepen their understanding of concepts. • enable them to visualize problems. • explore consequences of varying the data given.
6. Use Precise Mathematical Language Mathematically proficient students communicate precisely to others. They use clear definitions, including correct mathematical language, in discussion with others and in their own reasoning. They state the meaning of the symbols they choose, including using the equal sign consistently and appropriately. They express solutions clearly and logically by using the appropriate mathematical terms and notation. They specify units of measure and label axes to clarify the correspondence with quantities in a problem. They calculate accurately and efficiently and check the validity of their results in the context of the problem. They express numerical answers with a degree of precision appropriate for the problem context.	Math Talk Grade 1, Lesson 12.1 Grade 2, Lesson 5.4	**Children learn to:** • communicate precisely. • use mathematical vocabulary to communicate their ideas and explanations and to justify their thinking and solutions.
	Skill Lessons on number sentences and comparisons Grade K, Lesson 5.7 Grade 1, Lesson 7.4 Grade 2, Lesson 2.12	**Children learn to:** • state the meaning of the symbols $(+, -, <, >, =)$ they use in mathematical expressions and sentences accurately. • use the equal sign appropriately. • calculate accurately. • use comparison symbols $(<, >)$ appropriately.
	Measurement Lessons Grade 2, Lesson 8.6	**Children learn to:** • use correct measurement units for solutions.

Teacher Edition   Student Edition

Math Processes and Practices	Throughout *Go Math!* Look for...	Explanation
7. See Structure Mathematically proficient students look closely to discern a pattern or structure. They step back for an overview and shift perspective. They recognize and use properties of operations and equality. They organize and classify geometric shapes based on their attributes. They see expressions, equations, and geometric figures as single objects or as being composed of several objects.	**Some Examples:** Lessons with patterns Grade K, Lesson 9.11 Grade 1, Lesson 6.1 Grade 2, Lesson 1.8	**Children learn to:** • sort shapes according to attributes. • use mathematical vocabulary to communicate their ideas and explanations and to justify their thinking and solutions. • use familiar patterns in our number system to extend counting sequences.
	Geometry Lessons Grade 1, Lesson 11.4 Grade 2, Lesson 11.3	**Children learn to:** • verify that a new three-dimensional shape can be composed by combining three-dimensional shapes. • recognize and identify shapes by the number of side and vertices. • apply the structure of the base-ten number system to deeper understanding of the values of multi-digit numbers.
	Lessons with basic facts Grade 1, Lesson 3.6 Grade 2, Lesson 3.7	**Children learn to:** • use a variety of different strategies to find the sums and differences of basic facts. • use benchmark number 10 when finding differences.
8. Generalize Mathematically proficient students notice if calculations are repeated and look for general methods and shortcuts. They notice regularity in mathematical problems and their work to create a rule or formula. Mathematically proficient students maintain oversight of the process, while attending to the details as they solve a problem. They continually evaluate the reasonableness of their intermediate results.	Lessons with basic facts Grade K, Lesson 6.7 Grade 1, Lesson 5.2 Grade 2, Lesson 3.3	**Children learn to:** • find patterns in basic-fact strategies, such as the 'make a ten' 'doubles plus 1' and 'double minus 1'. • see the relationship between addition and subtraction. • recognize how structure and calculations are repeated as they build fact families. • discover shortcuts for finding sums of basic facts and for recognizing counting patterns.
	Multi-digit Computation Lessons Grade 1, Lesson 8.8 Grade 2, Lesson 6.7	**Children learn to:** • repeat the same steps for each place-value position in the standard algorithm for multi-digit computation.
	Lessons on Comparing Numbers Grade K, Lesson 4.7 Grade 1, Lesson 7.3 Grade 2, Lesson 2.12	**Children learn to:** • model and compare numbers to determine which is less or greater.

Teacher Edition   Student Edition

Big Idea

Extend conceptual understanding of number relationships and place value.

Number Sense and Place Value

Vocabulary Reader: Whales . . . . SE—1 . . . . . TE—1–4
Real World Project: By The Sea . . . . TE—8B

		STUDENT RESOURCES	TEACHER RESOURCES
1	**Number Concepts**	SE—9	. . . TE—9
✓	Show What You Know	SE—10	. . . . . TE—10
1	Hands On: **Algebra** • Even and Odd Numbers	SE—13	. . . . . TE—13A
2	**Algebra** • Represent Even Numbers	SE—19	. . . . . TE—19A
3	Understand Place Value	SE—25	. . . . . TE—25A
4	Expanded Form	SE—31	. . . . . TE—31A
5	Different Ways to Write Numbers	SE—37	. . . . . TE—37A
✓	Mid-Chapter Checkpoint	SE—40	. . . . . TE—40
6	**Algebra** • Different Names for Numbers	SE—43	. . . . . TE—43A
7	**Problem Solving** • Tens and Ones	SE—49	. . . . . TE—49A
8	Counting Patterns Within 100	SE—55	. . . . . TE—55A
9	Counting Patterns Within 1,000	SE—61	. . . . . TE—61A
✓	Chapter 1 Review/Test	SE—67	. . . . TE—67–68

Personal Math Trainer

Look for this symbol for a gateway to your personalized learning path!

2	**Numbers to 1,000**	SE—71	. . . TE—71
✓	Show What You Know	SE—72	. . . . . TE—72
1	Group Tens as Hundreds	SE—75	. . . . . TE—75A
2	Explore 3-Digit Numbers	SE—81	. . . . . TE—81A
3	Hands On • Model 3-Digit Numbers	SE—87	. . . . . TE—87A
4	Hundreds, Tens, and Ones	SE—93	. . . . . TE—93A
5	Place Value to 1,000	SE—99	. . . . . TE—99A
6	Number Names	SE—105	. . . . TE—105A
7	Different Forms of Numbers	SE—111	. . . . TE—111A
✓	Mid-Chapter Checkpoint	SE—114	. . . . TE—114
8	**Algebra** • Different Ways to Show Numbers	SE—117	. . . . TE—117A
9	Count On and Count Back by 10 and 100	SE—123	. . . . TE—123A
10	**Algebra** • Number Patterns	SE—129	. . . . TE—129A
11	**Problem Solving** • Compare Numbers	SE—135	. . . . TE—135A
12	**Algebra** • Compare Numbers	SE—141	. . . . TE—141A
✓	Chapter 2 Review/Test	SE—147	. . . . TE—147–148

Addition and Subtraction

Vocabulary Reader: All About Animals. . . . . . . SE—**151**. . TE—**151–154**

(Real World) Project: A Bunch of Animals . . . . TE—**158B**

		STUDENT RESOURCES	TEACHER RESOURCES
3	**Basic Facts and Relationships**	SE—**159**	TE—**159**
✓	Show What You Know.	SE—**160**	TE—**160**
1	Use Doubles Facts.	SE—**163**	TE—**163A**
2	Practice Addition Facts.	SE—**169**	TE—**169A**
3	Algebra • Make a Ten to Add	SE—**175**	TE—**175A**
4	Algebra • Add 3 Addends	SE—**181**	TE—**181A**
5	Algebra • Relate Addition and Subtraction	SE—**187**	TE—**187A**
6	Practice Subtraction Facts	SE—**193**	TE—**193A**
✓	Mid-Chapter Checkpoint.	SE—**196**	TE—**196**
7	Use Ten to Subtract	SE—**199**	TE—**199A**
8	Algebra • Use Drawings to Represent Problems	SE—**205**	TE—**205A**
9	Algebra • Use Equations to Represent Problems	SE—**211**	TE—**211A**
10	Problem Solving • Equal Groups.	SE—**217**	TE—**217A**
11	Algebra • Repeated Addition	SE—**223**	TE—**223A**
✓	Chapter 3 Review/Test.	SE—**229**	TE—**229–230**

Big Idea

Develop fluency with addition and subtraction within 100. Solve addition and subtraction problems within 1,000.

Math Processes and Practices

1. Problem Solving
2. Abstract and Quantitative Reasoning
3. Use and Evaluate Logical Reasoning
4. Mathematical Modeling
5. Use Mathematical Tools
6. Use Precise Mathematical Language
7. See Structure
8. Generalize

Key: SE—Student Edition; **TE**—Teacher Edition

Personal Math Trainer

Look for this symbol for a gateway to your personalized learning path!

		STUDENT RESOURCES	TEACHER RESOURCES
4	**2-Digit Addition**	SE—**233** . .	TE—**233**
✓	Show What You Know.	SE—**234**	TE—**234**
1	Break Apart Ones to Add.	SE—**237**	TE—**237A**
2	Use Compensation	SE—**243**	TE—**243A**
3	Break Apart Addends as Tens and Ones	SE—**249**	TE—**249A**
4	Model Regrouping for Addition	SE—**255**	TE—**255A**
5	Model and Record 2-Digit Addition	SE—**261**	TE—**261A**
6	2-Digit Addition	SE—**267**	TE—**267A**
7	Practice 2-Digit Addition	SE—**273**	TE—**273A**
✓	Mid-Chapter Checkpoint	SE—**276**	TE—**276**
8	Rewrite 2-Digit Addition	SE—**279**	TE—**279A**
9	Problem Solving • Addition.	SE—**285**	TE—**285A**
10	Algebra • Write Equations to Represent Addition	SE—**291**	TE—**291A**
11	Algebra • Find Sums for 3 Addends	SE—**297**	TE—**297A**
12	Algebra • Find Sums for 4 Addends	SE—**303**	TE—**303B**
✓	Chapter 4 Review/Test.	SE—**309**	TE—**309–310**

© Houghton Mifflin Harcourt Publishing Company • Image Credits: (l) Photodisc/Getty Images

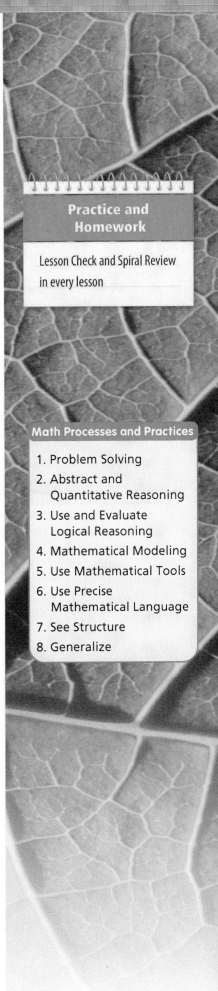

	STUDENT RESOURCES	TEACHER RESOURCES

5 2-Digit Subtraction . . . . SE—**313** . . TE—**313**

√ Show What You Know . . . . SE—**314** . . . . TE—**314**
1 Algebra • Break Apart Ones to Subtract . . . . SE—**317** . . . . TE—**317A**
2 Algebra • Break Apart Numbers to Subtract . . . . SE—**323** . . . . TE—**323A**
3 Model Regrouping for Subtraction . . . . SE—**329** . . . . TE—**329A**
4 Model and Record 2-Digit Subtraction . . . . SE—**335** . . . . TE—**335A**
5 2-Digit Subtraction . . . . SE—**341** . . . . TE—**341A**
6 Practice 2-Digit Subtraction . . . . SE—**347** . . . . TE—**347A**
√ Mid-Chapter Checkpoint . . . . SE—**350** . . . . TE—**350**
7 Rewrite 2-Digit Subtraction . . . . SE—**353** . . . . TE—**353A**
8 Add to Find Differences . . . . SE—**359** . . . . TE—**359A**
9 Problem Solving • Subtraction . . . . SE—**365** . . . . TE—**365A**
10 Algebra • Write Equations to Represent Subtraction . SE—**371** . . . . TE—**371A**
11 Solve Multistep Problems . . . . SE—**377** . . . . TE—**377A**
√ Chapter 5 Review/Test . . . . SE—**383** . . . . TE—**383–384**

6 3-Digit Addition and Subtraction . . . . SE—**387** . . TE—**387**

√ Show What You Know . . . . SE—**388** . . . . TE—**388**
1 Draw to Represent 3-Digit Addition . . . . SE—**391** . . . . TE—**391A**
2 Break Apart 3-Digit Addends . . . . SE—**397** . . . . TE—**397A**
3 3-Digit Addition: Regroup Ones . . . . SE—**403** . . . . TE—**403A**
4 3-Digit Addition: Regroup Tens . . . . SE—**409** . . . . TE—**409A**
5 Addition: Regroup Ones and Tens . . . . SE—**415** . . . . TE—**415A**
√ Mid-Chapter Checkpoint . . . . SE—**418** . . . . TE—**418**
6 Problem Solving • 3-Digit Subtraction . . . . SE—**421** . . . . TE—**421A**
7 3-Digit Subtraction: Regroup Tens . . . . SE—**427** . . . . TE—**427A**
8 3-Digit Subtraction: Regroup Hundreds . . . . SE—**433** . . . . TE—**433A**
9 Subtraction: Regroup Hundreds and Tens . . . . SE—**439** . . . . TE—**439A**
10 Regrouping with Zeros . . . . SE—**445** . . . . TE—**445A**
√ Chapter 6 Review/Test . . . . SE—**451** . . . . TE—**451–452**

Practice and Homework

Lesson Check and Spiral Review in every lesson

Math Processes and Practices

1. Problem Solving
2. Abstract and Quantitative Reasoning
3. Use and Evaluate Logical Reasoning
4. Mathematical Modeling
5. Use Mathematical Tools
6. Use Precise Mathematical Language
7. See Structure
8. Generalize

Key: SE—Student Edition; **TE**—Teacher Edition

© Houghton Mifflin Harcourt Publishing Company • Image Credits: (r) Photodisc/Getty Images

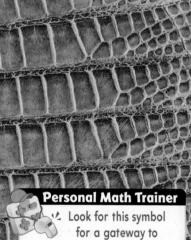

Big Idea

Use standard units of measure and extend conceptual understanding of time, data, and graphs. Develop a conceptual understanding of money.

Personal Math Trainer

Look for this symbol for a gateway to your personalized learning path!

Measurement and Data

Vocabulary Reader: Making a Kite . . . . SE—**455** . . TE—**455–456**

Project: Flying a Kite . . . . TE—**462B**

		STUDENT RESOURCES	TEACHER RESOURCES
7	**Money and Time**	SE—**463**	TE—**463**

✓ Show What You Know. SE—**464** . . . . TE—**464A**
1 Dimes, Nickels, and Pennies. . . . . SE—**467** . . . . TE—**467A**
2 Quarters . . . . SE—**473** . . . . TE—**473A**
3 Count Collections . . . . SE—**479** . . . . TE—**479A**
4 Hands On • Show Amounts in Two Ways . . . . SE—**485** . . . . TE—**485A**
5 One Dollar. . . . . SE—**491** . . . . TE—**491A**
✓ Mid-Chapter Checkpoint . . . . SE—**494** . . . . TE—**494**
6 Amounts Greater Than $1 . . . . SE—**497** . . . . TE—**497A**
7 Problem Solving • Money . . . . SE—**503** . . . . TE—**503A**
8 Time to the Hour and Half Hour . . . . SE—**509** . . . . TE—**509A**
9 Time to 5 Minutes . . . . SE—**515** . . . . TE—**515A**
10 Practice Telling Time. . . . . SE—**521** . . . . TE—**521A**
11 A.M. and P.M.. . . . . SE—**527** . . . . TE—**527A**
✓ Chapter 7 Review/Test. . . . . SE—**533** . . . . TE—**533–534**

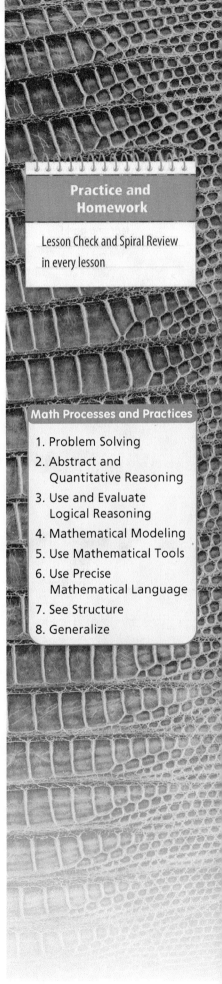

		STUDENT RESOURCES	TEACHER RESOURCES

8 Length in Customary Units . . . . SE—**537** . . TE—**537**

√ Show What You Know. . . . . SE—**538** . . . . TE—**538**

1 Hands On • Measure With Inch Models . . . . SE—**541** . . . . TE—**541A**

2 Hands On • Make and Use a Ruler . . . . SE—**547** . . . . TE—**547A**

3 Estimate Lengths in Inches. SE—**553** . . . . TE—**553A**

4 Hands On • Measure with an Inch Ruler. . . . . SE—**559** . . . . TE—**559A**

5 Problem Solving • Add and Subtract in Inches. . . . . . . SE—**565** . . . . TE—**565A**

√ Mid-Chapter Checkpoint . . . . SE—**568** . . . . TE—**568**

6 Hands On • Measure in Inches and Feet. . . . . SE—**571** . . . . TE—**571A**

7 Estimate Lengths in Feet . . . . SE—**577** . . . . TE—**577A**

8 Choose a Tool . . . . SE—**583** . . . . TE—**583A**

9 Display Measurement Data . . . . SE—**589** . . . . TE—**589A**

√ Chapter 8 Review/Test. . . . . SE—**595** . . . . TE—**595–596**

Practice and Homework

Lesson Check and Spiral Review in every lesson

Math Processes and Practices

1. Problem Solving
2. Abstract and Quantitative Reasoning
3. Use and Evaluate Logical Reasoning
4. Mathematical Modeling
5. Use Mathematical Tools
6. Use Precise Mathematical Language
7. See Structure
8. Generalize

Key: SE—Student Edition; **TE**—Teacher Edition

Personal Math Trainer

Look for this symbol for a gateway to your personalized learning path!

		STUDENT RESOURCES	TEACHER RESOURCES
9	**Length in Metric Units**	SE—**599**	TE—**599**
✓	Show What You Know	SE—**600**	TE—**600**
1	Hands On • Measure with a Centimeter Model	SE—**603**	TE—**603A**
2	Estimate Lengths in Centimeters	SE—**609**	TE—**609A**
3	Hands On • Measure with a Centimeter Ruler	SE—**615**	TE—**615A**
4	Problem Solving • Add and Subtract Lengths	SE—**621**	TE—**621A**
✓	Mid-Chapter Checkpoint	SE—**624**	TE—**624**
5	Hands On • Centimeters and Meters	SE—**627**	TE—**627A**
6	Estimate Lengths in Meters	SE—**633**	TE—**633A**
7	Hands On • Measure and Compare Lengths	SE—**639**	TE—**639A**
✓	Chapter 9 Review/Test	SE—**645**	TE—**645–646**
10	**Data**	SE—**649**	TE—**649**
✓	Show What You Know	SE—**650**	TE—**650**
1	Collect Data	SE—**653**	TE—**653A**
2	Read Picture Graphs	SE—**659**	TE—**659A**
3	Make Picture Graphs	SE—**665**	TE—**665A**
✓	Mid-Chapter Checkpoint	SE—**668**	TE—**668**
4	Read Bar Graphs	SE—**671**	TE—**671A**
5	Make Bar Graphs	SE—**677**	TE—**677A**
6	Problem Solving • Display Data	SE—**683**	TE—**683A**
✓	Chapter 10 Review/Test	SE—**689**	TE—**689–690**

Geometry and Fractions

Vocabulary Reader: A Farmer's Job. . . . . SE—**693** . . TE—**693**
Project: At the Farm Stand . . . . TE—**700B**

	STUDENT RESOURCES	TEACHER RESOURCES
11 Geometry	SE—**701**	TE—**701**
✓ Show What You Know.	SE—**702**	TE—**702**
1 Three-Dimensional Shapes.	SE—**705**	TE—**705A**
2 Attributes of Three-Dimensional Shapes	SE—**711**	TE—**711A**
3 Build Three-Dimensional Shapes.	SE—**717**	TE—**717A**
4 Two-Dimensional Shapes	SE—**723**	TE—**723A**
5 Angles in Two-Dimensional Shapes.	SE—**729**	TE—**729A**
6 Sort Two-Dimensional Shapes	SE—**735**	TE—**735A**
7 Hands On • Partition Rectangles.	SE—**741**	TE—**741A**
✓ Mid-Chapter Checkpoint	SE—**744**	TE—**744**
8 Equal Parts	SE—**747**	TE—**747A**
9 Show Equal Parts of a Whole.	SE—**753**	TE—**753A**
10 Describe Equal Parts.	SE—**759**	TE—**759A**
11 Problem Solving • Equal Shares	SE—**765**	TE—**765A**
✓ Chapter 11 Review/Test.	SE—**771**	TE—**771–772**

Big Idea
Describe, analyze, and draw two- and three-dimensional shapes. Develop a conceptual understanding of fractions.

Practice and Homework
Lesson Check and Spiral Review in every lesson

Math Processes and Practices
1. Problem Solving
2. Abstract and Quantitative Reasoning
3. Use and Evaluate Logical Reasoning
4. Mathematical Modeling
5. Use Mathematical Tools
6. Use Precise Mathematical Language
7. See Structure
8. Generalize

© Houghton Mifflin Harcourt Publishing Company • Image Credits: (r) ©Artville/Getty Images

Key: SE—Student Edition; **TE**—Teacher Edition

End-of-Year Resources

Projects

	STUDENT RESOURCES	TEACHER RESOURCES
Review Project: Books For Sale	P—B9	PG—PG42
Review Project: Plan a Trip to the Zoo	P—B13	PG—PG44
Review Project: Measuring Up!	P—B17	PG—PG46
Review Project: Shape Designs	P—B21	PG—PG48

Getting Ready for Grade 3

1 Find Sums on an Addition Table	Online	PG—PG50
2 Estimate Sums: 2-Digit Addition	Online	PG—PG52
3 Estimate Sums: 3-Digit Addition	Online	PG—PG54
4 Estimate Differences: 2-Digit Subtraction	Online	PG—PG56
5 Estimate Differences: 3-Digit Subtraction	Online	PG—PG58
6 Order 3-Digit Numbers	Online	PG—PG60
✓ Checkpoint	Online	PG—PG61
7 Equal Groups of 2	Online	PG—PG62
8 Equal Groups of 5	Online	PG—PG64
9 Equal Groups of 10	Online	PG—PG66
10 Hands On • Size of Shares	Online	PG—PG68
11 Hands On • Number of Equal Shares	Online	PG—PG70
12 Solve Problems with Equal Shares	Online	PG—PG72
✓ Checkpoint	Online	PG—PG73
✓ Getting Ready Test • Lessons 1–12	Online	PG—PG74
13 Hour Before and Hour After	Online	PG—PG76
14 Elapsed Time in Hours	Online	PG—PG78
15 Elapsed Time in Minutes	Online	PG—PG80
16 Hands On: Capacity • Nonstandard Units	Online	PG—PG82
17 Describe Measurement Data	Online	PG—PG84
✓ Checkpoint	Online	PG—PG85
18 Fraction Models: Thirds and Sixths	Online	PG—PG86
19 Fraction Models: Fourths and Eighths	Online	PG—PG88
20 Compare Fraction Models	Online	PG—PG90
✓ Checkpoint	Online	PG—PG91
✓ Getting Ready Test • Lessons 13–20	Online	PG—PG92

Key: P—Online Projects; PG—Planning Guide

Teacher Notes

Online Projects

Review Project:

Books For Sale

BIG IDEA Extend conceptual understanding of number relationships and place value.

Print Resources

• Planning Guide, p. PG42

Review Project:

Plan a Trip to the Zoo

BIG IDEA Develop fluency with addition and subtraction within 100. Solve addition and subtraction problems within 1,000.

Print Resources

• Planning Guide, p. PG44

Review Project:

Measuring Up!

BIG IDEA Use standard units of measure and extend conceptual understanding of time, data, and graphs. Develop a conceptual understanding of money.

Print Resources

• Planning Guide, p. PG46

Review Project:

Shape Designs

BIG IDEA Describe, analyze, and draw two- and three-dimensional shapes. Develop a conceptual understanding of fractions.

Print Resources

• Planning Guide, p. PG48

 Animated Math Models

✓ Assessment

〜 HMH Mega Math

iT iTools

P Projects

ABC Multimedia eGlossary

Getting Ready Lessons build on Grade 2 content and prepare students for Grade 3 content.

Daily Pacing Chart

Review Projects	Lessons	Assessment	Total
4 days	20 days	2 days	26 days

LESSON 1 **Find Sums On An Addition Table**

Resources

• Student Lesson Pages, Online
• Planning Guide, p. PG50

LESSON 5 **Estimate Differences: 3-Digit Subtraction**

Resources

• Student Lesson Pages, Online
• Planning Guide, p. PG58

LESSON 6 **Order 3-Digit Numbers**

Resources

• Student Lesson Pages, Online
• Planning Guide, p. PG60

LESSON 10 HANDS ON: **Size Of Shares**

Resources

• Student Lesson Pages, Online
• Planning Guide, p. PG68

LESSON 11 HANDS ON: **Number Of Equal Shares**

Resources

• Student Lesson Pages, Online
• Planning Guide, p. PG70

LESSON 15 **Elapsed Time In Minutes**

Resources

• Student Lesson Pages, Online
• Planning Guide, p. PG80

LESSON 16 HANDS ON: **Capacity • Nonstandard Units**

Resources

• Student Lesson Pages, Online
• Planning Guide, p. PG82

LESSON 20 **Compare Fraction Models**

Resources

• Student Lesson Pages, Online
• Planning Guide, p. PG90

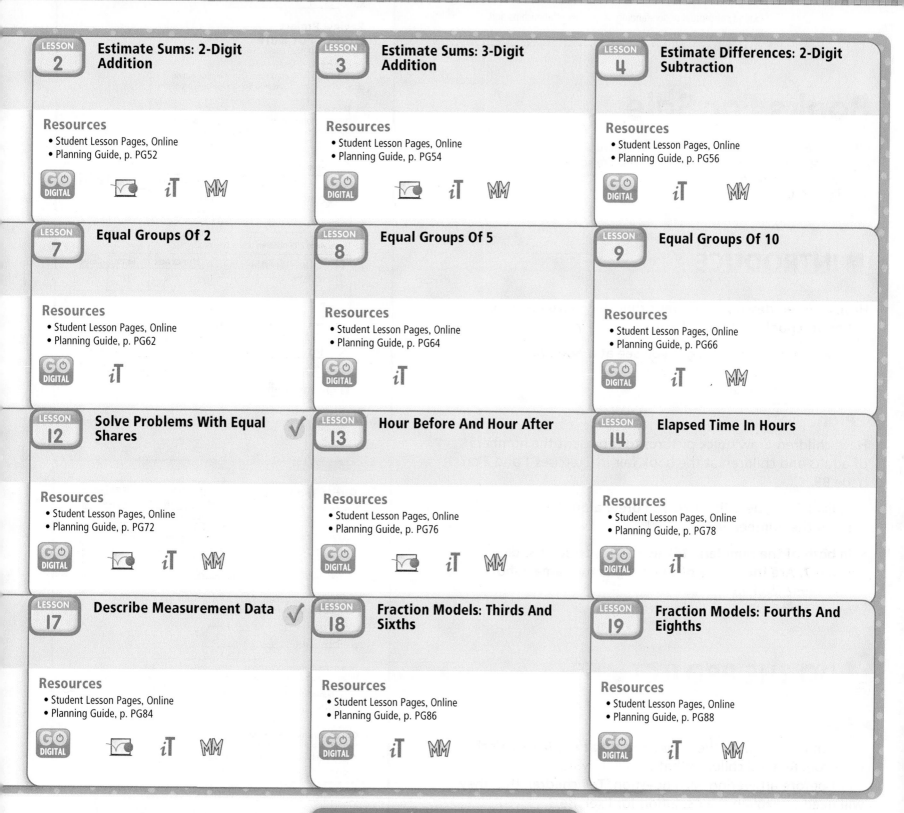

LESSON 2 — Estimate Sums: 2-Digit Addition

Resources
- Student Lesson Pages, Online
- Planning Guide, p. PG52

LESSON 3 — Estimate Sums: 3-Digit Addition

Resources
- Student Lesson Pages, Online
- Planning Guide, p. PG54

LESSON 4 — Estimate Differences: 2-Digit Subtraction

Resources
- Student Lesson Pages, Online
- Planning Guide, p. PG56

LESSON 7 — Equal Groups Of 2

Resources
- Student Lesson Pages, Online
- Planning Guide, p. PG62

LESSON 8 — Equal Groups Of 5

Resources
- Student Lesson Pages, Online
- Planning Guide, p. PG64

LESSON 9 — Equal Groups Of 10

Resources
- Student Lesson Pages, Online
- Planning Guide, p. PG66

LESSON 12 — Solve Problems With Equal Shares

Resources
- Student Lesson Pages, Online
- Planning Guide, p. PG72

LESSON 13 — Hour Before And Hour After

Resources
- Student Lesson Pages, Online
- Planning Guide, p. PG76

LESSON 14 — Elapsed Time In Hours

Resources
- Student Lesson Pages, Online
- Planning Guide, p. PG78

LESSON 17 — Describe Measurement Data

Resources
- Student Lesson Pages, Online
- Planning Guide, p. PG84

LESSON 18 — Fraction Models: Thirds And Sixths

Resources
- Student Lesson Pages, Online
- Planning Guide, p. PG86

LESSON 19 — Fraction Models: Fourths And Eighths

Resources
- Student Lesson Pages, Online
- Planning Guide, p. PG88

✔ Assessment

An Assessment Check Mark following a lesson title indicates that a Checkpoint or Getting Ready Test is available for assessment after completing the lesson.

Checkpoints and Getting Ready Tests can be found in the online Getting Ready Lessons and Resources.

Extend conceptual understanding of number relationships and place value.

●●

Books For Sale

Objective
Apply place value concepts to represent and to compare multidigit numbers.

Materials
Online Project pp. B9–B12

① INTRODUCE

Have children describe book fairs that they have been to, either at school or at special events.

- **What kinds of books might you see at a book fair?** Possible answers: books about animals, space books, sports books, cookbooks, chapter books, coloring books

▶ Plan

Have children draw quick pictures to represent the numbers of adults and children at the book fair in Exercises 1 and 2 on page B9.

- **In Exercise 1, describe how you drew a quick picture to show the number 147.** Check children's answers for understanding.

- **In both of the numbers, 147 and 704, you see the digits 4 and 7. Are the values of these digits the same in both numbers? Explain.** No. Possible explanation: The values of the digits are different because they are in different place value positions for each number.

② DO THE PROJECT

▶ Put It Together

Have children look at the *Books Bought at the Book Fair* chart with you. Remind children that they will need to refer to the chart before answering each question. Tell children that they will need to explain their solution for Exercise 3.

Name _____

Review Project
Books For Sale
See Planning Guide • End-of-Year Resources for Lesson Plans.

Project
Many schools have book fairs. Use the information about a book fair at Lakeside School to solve problems.

▶ Plan
Draw quick pictures to show how many adults and how many children went to the book fair. Then write how many hundreds, tens, and ones.

1. There were 147 adults at the book fair.

Check children's drawings.

Hundreds	Tens	Ones
1	4	7

2. There were 704 children at the book fair.

Check children's drawings.

Hundreds	Tens	Ones
7	0	4

3. Were there more children than adults at the book fair? Explain.

Yes. Possible answer: I compared the hundreds first. 7 hundreds is more than 1 hundred, so 704 is greater than 147.

Review Project   B9

▶ Put It Together
Use this information about books that were bought at the book fair.

Books Bought at the Book Fair

Kind of Book	Number
people	225
animals	303
space	59
history	167
games	85

1. How many books about animals were bought? Write the number two different ways.

 __3__ hundreds __0__ tens __3__ ones

 __300__ + __0__ + __3__

2. How many books about history were bought? Write the number two different ways.

 __1__ hundred __6__ tens __7__ ones

 __100__ + __60__ + __7__

3. Compare the number of books about animals to the number of books about games. Which number of books is greater? Explain.

 __303__ ⟩ __85__ , or 85 < 303

 More books about animals were bought.

 Possible explanation: I compared 303 and 85. I started with the hundreds. 303 has 3 hundreds. 85 has 0 hundreds. 3 is greater than 0. So, 303 books is greater than 85 books.

B10

Name _____

Reflect

Use the information about the books to complete each sentence. Write the comparison.

Books Bought at the Book Fair	
Kind of Book	**Number**
people	225
animals	303
space	59
history	167
games	85

For exercises 1–2, answers may vary. Possible answers are given.

1. More books about ___**people**___ than books about ___**history**___ were bought.

2. Fewer books about ___**space**___ than books about ___**games**___ were bought.

3. Order from greatest to least the number of books bought about people, animals, and history.

   ___303___ ⊘ ___225___ ⊘ ___167___

4. For which kinds of books were there fewer than 100 books bought? Explain how you know.

   space and games; Possible explanation:

   The numbers of books bought about space

   and games only have tens and ones digits,

   so both numbers are less than 100.

Review Project   **B11**

Go Beyond

Choose the number from the box that best answers each question.

361	258
58	
180	67

1. Alex bought a book that had fewer than 60 pages. How many pages could the book have?

   ___58___ pages

2. Jennie bought a book that had more than 150 pages but fewer than 200 pages. How many pages could the book have?

   ___180___ pages

Write the missing digit to complete the comparison. For exercises 3–8, some possible answers are given.

3. 345 > 3 _4_ 0   4. 273 < 27 _4_   5. 8 _6_ 3 > 862

6. 5 _4_ 5 < 550   7. 633 > 63 _2_   8. 12 _4_ < 125

9. For Exercise 3, what other digits could you have used? Explain.

   Possible digits are 4, 3, 2, 1, or 0. With these

   digits, the number would be 340, 330, 320, 310,

   or 300. These numbers are all less than 345.

B12

Reflect

Tell children that there is more than one possible answer for Exercise 1 and for Exercise 2. You might challenge children to write comparisons (such as 225 > 167) to represent their solutions to these exercises.

Go Beyond

Have children identify each of the numbers in the box at the top right corner of the page.

For Exercises 3–8, children must write a missing digit to correctly complete each comparison. In Exercise 9, children are asked to list other digits and explain why they could have been used to solve Exercise 3.

③ EXTEND THE PROJECT

Work as a class to make a booklet called *Library Riddles, Puzzles, and Stories*. Have children write riddles about different library-related things. The numbers of things should be 3-digit numbers and the riddles should have clues about place value. They can also use 3-digit numbers to write stories and puzzles about the library.

Portfolio You can use this project as a means of assessing a child's understanding of the concepts and skills found in this Big Idea.

Performance Assessment

Project Scoring Rubric

3 Demonstrates a full understanding of the project. Correctly models, compares, and orders numbers.

2 Demonstrates a thorough understanding of the project. Models, compares, and orders with one or two errors.

1 Demonstrates a partial understanding of the project. Models, compares, and orders numbers with some errors.

0 Demonstrates little understanding of the project. Incorrectly models, compares, and orders most numbers.

Develop fluency with addition and subtraction within 100. Solve addition and subtraction problems within 1,000.

Plan a Trip to the Zoo

Objective
Develop fluency with multidigit addition and subtraction.

Materials
Online Project pp. B13–B16

1 INTRODUCE

Ask children if they have ever gone on a school trip.

- **Where did you go?**
- **How did you get there?**
- **Who went on the trip?**

Discuss plans that might need to be made for a class trip.

▶ Plan

Tell children that they will help plan a second grade trip to the zoo. Discuss things they will need to know to plan the trip. Then work together to answer the questions on page B13. Remind children to be sure to count themselves when they find the answers for Exercise 1.

- **How can you find the total number of boys and girls in the class?** Add the number of girls to the number of boys.

- **Look at Exercise 3. Describe how you will compare the numbers of boys and girls.** Possible answer: I will compare the tens digits first. If the tens digits are the same, then I will compare the ones digits. **Describe how you will find how many more boys than girls [or girls than boys] there are.** Possible answer: I will subtract.

2 DO THE PROJECT

▶ Put It Together

Children can refer to page B13 to complete the left column in the chart on page B14. For the right column of the chart, provide children with the numbers of boys and girls in another second grade class. Tell children they will use the information in the chart to solve Exercises 1 and 2.

- **How can you find the total number of girls?** Add the number of girls in our class to the number of girls in the other second grade class.

Children may use a drawing and a counting pattern to help them find the answer to Exercise 3.

Name _____

Review Project
Plan a Trip to the Zoo
See Planning Guide • End-of-Year Resources for Lesson Plans.

Project

Suppose the second graders in your school are going on a trip to the zoo. Help plan the trip.

▶ **Plan**
First find out how many children in your class might go on the trip.

Check children's work.

1. How many girls are in your class? How many boys are in your class?

_____ girls   _____ boys

2. How many children in all are in your class?

_____ children

3. Are the numbers of boys and girls in your class the same? If not, are there more boys or more girls? How many more? Show your work.

_____
_____
_____

Review Project   B13

▶ **Put It Together**
Ask your teacher for the number of second graders who are in another class that might go on the trip. Complete the chart. Then answer each question. Show your work.

Check children's work.

Second Graders Going on the Trip	
Your Class	**Another Class**
_____ girls	_____ girls
_____ boys	_____ boys

1. What is the total number of girls?

_____ girls

2. What is the total number of boys?

_____ boys

3. Children will sit in rows of 5 children for the bird show. How many children will sit in the first 5 rows? Explain.

25 children; Possible explanation: I drew
a picture to show 5 rows of 5. Then I skip
counted by fives 5 times: 5, 10, 15, 20, 25. So,
25 children will sit in the first 5 rows.

B14

Name _____

▶ **Reflect**

Plan to take lunch to the zoo. Use the information from the chart on page B14. Show your work.

Check children's work.

1. Each child needs one sandwich. How many sandwiches will you need?

_____ sandwiches

2. You can bring peanut butter and jelly sandwiches and tuna fish sandwiches. How many of each could you bring to have enough?

_____ peanut butter and jelly sandwiches

_____ tuna fish sandwiches

3. Each child will get one morning snack and one afternoon snack. How many snacks will you need?

_____ snacks

Review Project   **B15**

Go Beyond

For every 8 children who go on the trip, there will be 1 adult. How many adults need to go on the trip? Draw or write to show how you got your answer.

Check children's work.

_____ adults

B16

Online Projects, pp. B15–B16

▶ **Reflect**

You may wish to have children work with a partner to solve each problem on page B15.

- **How can you find the total number of sandwiches needed for the trip?** Add the total number of girls going on the trip to the total number of boys going on the trip to find how many children are going.

If children are having difficulty with Exercise 2, explain that they are to find two numbers that have a sum that matches the number of sandwiches in Exercise 1.

▶ **Go Beyond**

You may wish to have pairs of children work together to solve the non-routine problem on page B16. Refer pairs to Exercise 1 on page B15 to find the number of children that will go on the trip.

If the total number of children going on the trip is not a multiple of 8, you may wish to tell the class that a group of children "left over" (fewer than 8 children after groups of 8 are made) would also need an adult. This means that the number of adults needed should increase by one.

③ EXTEND THE PROJECT

Have children write their own word problems involving addition and subtraction of 2- and 3-digit numbers. Problems might involve zoo animals, tickets for zoo rides, zoo souvenirs, and so on.

Portfolio ✓ You can use this project as a means of assessing a child's understanding of the concepts and skills found in this Big Idea.

Project Scoring Rubric

3 Demonstrates a full understanding of the project. Correctly adds and subtracts numbers to solve problems.

2 Demonstrates a thorough understanding of the project. Adds and subtracts numbers to solve problems with one or two errors.

1 Demonstrates a partial understanding of the project. Makes a good attempt, with some errors, at solving problems.

0 Demonstrates little understanding of the project. Incorrectly adds and subtracts numbers and provides inaccurate solutions.

Use standard units of measure and extend conceptual understanding of time, data, and graphs. Develop a conceptual understanding of money.

Measuring Up!

Objective
Measure lengths using customary and metric units.

Materials
Online Project pp. B17–B20, inch rulers, centimeter rulers, yardsticks, metersticks

1 INTRODUCE

Discuss the different measurement tools pictured on page B17. Explain to children that a balance and a measuring cup are used to measure weight and volume.

- **Describe a length that you would measure using a yardstick.** Possible answers: the length of our classroom, the distance from the school library to the playground

- **Which tool would you use to measure the length of a pencil?** Possible answers: centimeter ruler, inch ruler

Discuss how different tools are used to measure different things.

▶ Plan

Have children look at page B17 and identify each measurement tool. You may wish to ask children if they know of any other tools that could be used to measure length, height, and distance that are not pictured on page B17, such as a measuring tape. Encourage discussion on how these tools would be used.

2 DO THE PROJECT

▶ Put It Together

Have children work with a partner. Distribute inch rulers and centimeter rulers to pairs. Pairs can share yardsticks and metersticks if needed.

Have children look at page B18. Before children measure items for Exercises 1–3, encourage them to first determine the unit (inches, feet) they will use for each item.

For Exercises 4 and 5, remind children that they will use centimeter rulers and metersticks.

Name _____

▶ **Reflect**

Choose the unit and tool you would use to measure.
Explain your choices.

Units	inches	feet	
	centimeters	meters	
Tools	inch ruler	yardstick	measuring tape
	centimeter ruler	meterstick	

1. the height of your school

Possible answer: I would use feet and a
yardstick or meters and a meterstick because
my school is very tall.

2. the length of a book

Possible answer: I would use inches and an
inch ruler or centimeters and a centimeter ruler
because a book is much smaller than a yardstick
or a meterstick.

Which is a greater length? Circle it.

3.	5 centimeters	4.	**(3 feet)**	5.	**(2 meters)**
	or		or		or
	(5 meters)		3 inches		2 centimeters

Review Project   **B19**

▶ **Go Beyond**

Some friends rolled marbles to see how far the
marbles could go.
They measured the distance each marble rolled.
The bar graph shows the data. Use the bar
graph to answer the questions.

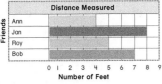

Distance Measured

Friends: Ann, Jan, Roy, Bob — Number of Feet (0 1 2 3 4 5 6 7 8 9)

1. Whose marble rolled the farthest distance? Whose rolled the
shortest distance?
Jan's marble rolled the farthest distance.
Ann's marble rolled the shortest distance.

2. How do the bars on the graph help you compare distances?
Possible answer: You can look at the lengths of
the bars to see which distance is longest and
which is shortest.

3. Why must all the distances be given in feet?
Possible answer: All the distances must be given
in feet so you can graph the distances correctly.
If they were in different units, you could not
show the distances on the same graph.
B20

Online Projects, pp. B19–B20

▶ **Reflect**

Have children complete Exercises 1 and 2 on page B19.

- **Suppose you measured the height of your school in
inches and then in feet. How would the measurements be
different? Explain.** Possible answer: The number of inches would be
greater than the number of feet because inches are shorter than feet, and
it would take more inches than feet to measure the school's height.

- **Suppose you want to measure the length of a baseball
card in centimeters. Could you use either a centimeter
ruler or a meterstick?** Yes. **Which tool do you think would
be better to use? Explain.** Possible answer: A smaller tool is easier
to use when measuring small items. A larger tool is easier to use when
measuring large items. I would use a centimeter ruler to measure the
length of a baseball card.

Exercises 3–5 check children's understanding of the relative
sizes of measurement units.

▶ **Go Beyond**

On page B20, children analyze measurement data displayed in
a bar graph. In Exercise 2, children think about how a bar graph
helps them to compare measurements.

③ EXTEND THE PROJECT

Have children estimate the length or height of various
classroom objects and then measure to check their estimates.
Remind them to choose the tool and unit they think is most
appropriate for measuring each object.

You can use this project as a means of assessing a
child's understanding of the concepts and skills found
in this Big Idea.

Performance Assessment

Project Scoring Rubric

3   Demonstrates a full understanding of the project.
Selects appropriate tools and measures accurately.

2   Demonstrates a thorough understanding of the project.
Selects appropriate tools and measures accurately with
one or two errors.

1   Demonstrates a partial understanding of the project.
Selects appropriate tools and measures accurately with
some errors.

0   Demonstrates little understanding of the project. Chooses
inappropriate measurement tools and measures incorrectly.

Describe, analyze, and draw two- and three-dimensional shapes.
Develop a conceptual understanding of fractions.

Shape Designs

Objective
Apply concepts of two-dimensional shapes.

Materials
Online Project pp. B21–B24, pattern blocks

1 INTRODUCE

Discuss the two-dimensional shapes shown on page B21. Have children identify the sides of the shape in Exercise 1.

- **What is an angle?** where two sides of a shape meet, they form an angle

▶ Plan

Ask children to identify and describe each shape on page B21.

- **How are the shapes in Exercises 1, 3, and 6 alike? How are they different?** Possible answer: These three shapes each have 4 sides and 4 angles. The shapes look different.

You may wish to discuss which pattern blocks can be put together to make other shapes. For example, children can arrange three triangle pattern blocks to make a trapezoid.

2 DO THE PROJECT

▶ Put It Together

Distribute pattern blocks to children. You may wish to have children work in pairs. Have children use the blocks to make a design on page B22. Tell children that the blocks should not have any overlaps. After they have made their design with the blocks, ask children to trace around the blocks to draw the design on the page.

Name _____

Review Project
Shape Designs

See Planning Guide •
End-of-Year Resources
for Lesson Plans.

Project
Bart wants to use two-dimensional shapes to draw a design for a poster. Help Bart make his design.

▶ **Plan**
Describe the shapes you might use for the design. Write how many sides and angles each shape has.

1.   __4__ sides __4__ angles

2.   __3__ sides __3__ angles

3.   __4__ sides __4__ angles

4.   __4__ sides __4__ angles

5.   __6__ sides __6__ angles

6.   __4__ sides __4__ angles

Review Project   B21

▶ **Put It Together**
Use pattern blocks. Draw a design for Bart. Trace the blocks.

Check children's work.

B22

Name _____

▶ **Reflect**
Answer the questions about your design.

Check children's work.

1. How many of each shape did you use?

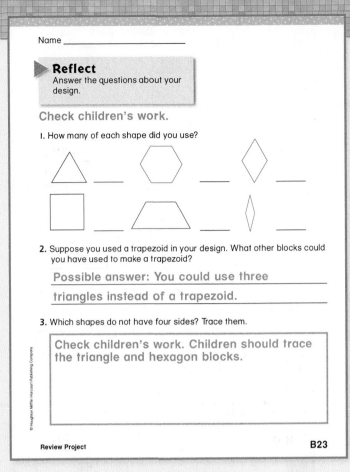

2. Suppose you used a trapezoid in your design. What other blocks could you have used to make a trapezoid?

Possible answer: You could use three triangles instead of a trapezoid.

3. Which shapes do not have four sides? Trace them.

Check children's work. Children should trace the triangle and hexagon blocks.

Review Project   B23

▶ **Go Beyond**
Here is a design that Ida drew.
What pattern block shapes could she have used?
Find different ways to arrange shapes.
Trace the ways.

Check children's work. Two ways are shown.

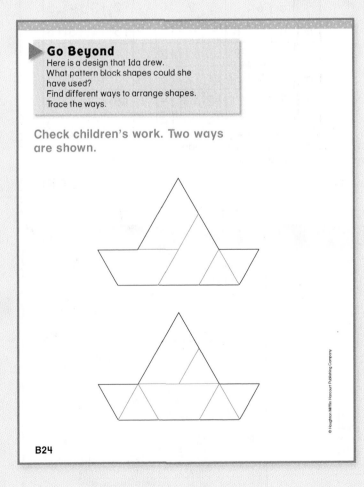

B24

▶ **Reflect**
Have children complete Exercises 1–3 on page B23. Have children refer to the designs that they drew on page B22 to answer Exercise 1. Ask volunteers to share their designs with the class.

▶ **Go Beyond**
On page B24, children identify smaller shapes that make up the large shape. They find two ways to arrange their pattern blocks to match the large shape. Have children analyze the designs on this page. Encourage children to use different types of pattern blocks for each way they arrange the blocks to match the large shapes.

③ EXTEND THE PROJECT

Have children identify classroom objects that match three-dimensional shapes, such as spheres, cones, cylinders, cubes, and other rectangular prisms. Then have children make a list of other real-life objects that match each three-dimensional shape.

Portfolio You can use this project as a means of assessing a child's understanding of the concepts and skills found in this Big Idea.

Project Scoring Rubric

3 Demonstrates a full understanding of the project. Correctly describes and analyzes the attributes of shapes.

2 Demonstrates a thorough understanding of the project. Describes and analyzes the attributes of the shapes with one or two errors.

1 Demonstrates a partial understanding of the project. Describes and analyzes the attributes of the shapes with errors.

0 Demonstrates little understanding of the project. Incorrectly describes and analyzes the attributes of most shapes.

LESSON 1

Find Sums on an Addition Table

LESSON AT A GLANCE

Lesson Objective
Find sums to 20 on an addition table.

Essential Question
How do you find sums on an addition table?

Materials
MathBoard, iTools: Number Charts [optional]

GO DIGITAL

iT iTools: Number Charts (Addition Chart)

1 TEACH and TALK GO DIGITAL • Animated Math Models

▶ **Model and Draw** Math Processes and Practices

Point out the addition problem at the top of the page, and discuss how to find the sum by using the addition table.

- **Find the addend 3 in the shaded column on the left side of the table. Where on the addition table will you look for the other addend?** in the shaded row on top of the table

- **Where on the addition table is the sum?** where row 3 and column 4 meet

2 PRACTICE MATH BOARD

▶ **Share and Show** • **Guided Practice**

- **How will you know which addends to use?** Look in the shaded row above and in the shaded column to the left of the missing sum.

Use **Math Talk** to focus on children's understanding of patterns in the addition table.

Name _____

Find Sums on an Addition Table

Essential Question How do you find sums on an addition table?

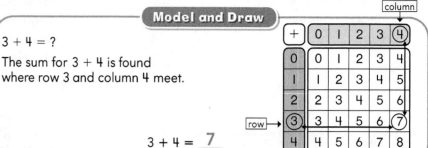

This lesson builds on addition within 20 presented in Chapter 3 and prepares children for identifying and explaining arithmetic patterns in the addition table taught in Grade 3.

Model and Draw

$3 + 4 = ?$

The sum for $3 + 4$ is found where row 3 and column 4 meet.

$3 + 4 = \underline{7}$

+	0	1	2	3	④
0	0	1	2	3	4
1	1	2	3	4	5
2	2	3	4	5	6
③	3	4	5	6	⑦
4	4	5	6	7	8

Share and Show MATH BOARD

1. Write the missing sums in the addition table.

+	0	1	2	3	4	5	6	7	8	9	10
0	0	1	2	3	4	5	6	7	8	9	10
1	1	2	3	4	5	6	7	8	9	10	11
2	2	3	4	5	6	7	8	9	10	11	12
3	3	4	5	6	7	8	9	10	11	12	13
4	4	5	6	7	8	9	10	11	12	13	14
5	5	6	7	8	9	10	11	12	13	14	15
6	6	7	8	9	10	11	12	13	14	15	16
7	7	8	9	10	11	12	13	14	15	16	17
8	8	9	10	11	12	13	14	15	16	17	18
9	9	10	11	12	13	14	15	16	17	18	19
10	10	11	12	13	14	15	16	17	18	19	20

 Math Talk Describe a pattern in the addition table. Answers will vary. Possible answer: The same sums are in a diagonal line in the table.

Getting Ready for Grade 3   one **GRI**

GR: Practice, p. GRP1

Name _____   Lesson 1

Find Sums on an Addition Table

1. Write the missing sums in the addition table.

Problem Solving

Solve. Write or draw to explain.

2. Marvin finds doubles facts, such as $4 + 4$ and $1 + 1$, on the addition table. He colors each sum.

What pattern does Marvin make when he colors the sums of the doubles facts?

Possible answer: Marvin colors a diagonal pattern from the upper left to the lower right.

Getting Ready for Grade 3   GRPI

GR: Reteach, p. GRR1

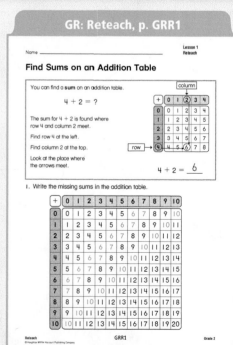

Name _____   Lesson 1
                                       Reteach

Find Sums on an Addition Table

You can find a **sum** on an addition table.

$4 + 2 = ?$

The sum for $4 + 2$ is found where row 4 and column 2 meet.

Find row 4 at the left.
Find column 2 at the top.
Look at the place where the arrows meet.

$4 + 2 = \underline{6}$

1. Write the missing sums in the addition table.

Reteach   GRR1   Grade 2

*GR – Getting Ready Lessons and Resources (*www.thinkcentral.com*)

On Your Own

2. Write the missing sums in the addition table.

+	0	1	2	3	4	5	6	7	8	9	10
0	0	1	2	3	4	5	6	7	8	9	10
1	1	2	3	4	5	6	7	8	9	10	11
2	2	3	4	5	6	7	8	9	10	11	12
3	3	4	5	6	7	8	9	10	11	12	13
4	4	5	6	7	8	9	10	11	12	13	14
5	5	6	7	8	9	10	11	12	13	14	15
6	6	7	8	9	10	11	12	13	14	15	16
7	7	8	9	10	11	12	13	14	15	16	17
8	8	9	10	11	12	13	14	15	16	17	18
9	9	10	11	12	13	14	15	16	17	18	19
10	10	11	12	13	14	15	16	17	18	19	20

Problem Solving

Solve. Write or draw to explain.

3. Natasha has 13 apples. Some apples are red and some are green. She has more red apples than green apples. How many red apples and how many green apples could she have?

Answers will vary. Some possible answers: 7 red and 6 green; 8 red and 5 green; 9 red and 4 green

 TAKE HOME ACTIVITY • Ask your child to explain how to use the addition table to find the sum of 8 + 6.

GR2 two

© Houghton Mifflin Harcourt Publishing Company

▶ **On Your Own** • Independent Practice

If children complete Exercise 1 correctly, assign Exercise 2. Suggest that children make use of any patterns they notice.

- **What pattern do you see in the boxes where you have written 11 as a missing sum? Why do you think this pattern happens?** Check children's answers for reasonableness. One possible answer: As you move from each box with a sum of 11, one of the addends increases by 1 and the other decreases by 1.

▶ **Problem Solving**

UNLOCK THE PROBLEM Read aloud the problem in Exercise 3. Discuss with children how they can use the addition table to solve the problem.

- **When you look at the addition table to find sums of 13, could you use any of these pairs of addends for your answer? Explain.** Yes; Possible explanation: In each pair of addends, one of the addends is greater than the other. So, I would need to use the greater addend for the number of red apples and the lesser addend for the number of green apples .

3 SUMMARIZE

Math Processes and Practices

Essential Question

How do you find sums on an addition table?
Possible answer: You find one addend in the shaded row and the other addend in the shaded column. The sum is found where that row and that column meet.

Math Journal  Math

Use the addition table to list some addition facts that have a sum of 15. Describe a pattern that you see in these facts.

LESSON 2

Estimate Sums: 2-Digit Addition

LESSON AT A GLANCE

Lesson Objective
Estimate sums of 2-digit numbers.

Essential Question
How can you estimate the sum of two 2-digit numbers?

Materials
MathBoard

- ☑ Animated Math Models
- *i*T *i*Tools: Number Line
- WW HMH Mega Math

---

1 TEACH and TALK 🔵 • Animated Math Models

▶ **Model and Draw** (Math Processes and Practices)

As you work through the model, remind children that they estimate to find *about* how many.

- **What numbers are shown on the number line?** numbers from 20 to 40
- **What does the arrow pointing to the 20 show you?** 20 is the nearest ten to 24. **What does the arrow pointing to the 40 show you?** 40 is the nearest ten to 38.
- **Why is 20 + 40 a reasonable way to estimate the sum of 24 + 38?** Possible answer: 20 and 40 are the nearest tens to 24 and 38, so the sum of 20 + 40 will be close to the actual sum of 24 + 38.

2 PRACTICE [MATH BOARD]

▶ **Share and Show** • Guided Practice

- **For Exercise 1, what will you do first to estimate the sum?** Possible answer: I will put points on the number line for 18 and 29, and then I will find the nearest ten for each number.

This lesson builds on 2-digit addition skills taught in Chapter 4 and prepares children for rounding numbers and estimating multi-digit sums taught in Grade 3.

Name _____

Estimate Sums: 2-Digit Addition

Essential Question How can you estimate the sum of two 2-digit numbers?

Model and Draw

Estimate the sum of 24 + 38.
Find the nearest ten for each number.

20 21 22 23 **24** 25 26 27 28 29 **30** 31 32 33 34 35 36 37 38 39 **40**

__20__ + __40__ = __60__

An estimate of the sum is __60__.

Share and Show [MATH BOARD]

Find the nearest ten for each number.

1. Estimate the sum of 18 + 29.

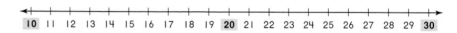

10 11 12 13 14 15 16 17 18 19 **20** 21 22 23 24 25 26 27 28 29 **30**

Add the tens to estimate.

__20__ + __30__ = __50__

An estimate of the sum is __50__.

 Math Talk How did you know which ten is nearest to 18?

Getting Ready for Grade 3

Possible answer: 18 is between 10 and 20. Looking at the number line, I can see that it is nearer to 20 than to 10.

three **GR3**

GR: Practice, p. GRP2

Name _____ **Lesson 2**

Estimate Sums: 2-Digit Addition

Find the nearest ten for each number.
Add the tens to estimate.

1. Estimate the sum of 21 + 17.

10 11 12 13 14 15 16 17 18 19 **20** 21 22 23 24 25 26 27 28 29 **30**

__20__ + __20__ = __40__
An estimate of the sum is __40__.

2. Estimate the sum of 32 + 49.

30 31 32 33 34 35 36 37 38 39 **40** 41 42 43 44 45 46 47 48 49 **50**

__30__ + __50__ = __80__
An estimate of the sum is __80__.

Problem Solving (Real World)

Solve. Write or draw to explain.   Possible answer is given.

3. Taryn had 38 marbles. Her sister gave her 29 more marbles. Estimate the number of marbles Taryn has now.

about __70__ marbles

Getting Ready for Grade 3   GRP2

GR: Reteach, p. GRR2

Name _____   Lesson 2 Reteach

Estimate Sums: 2-Digit Addition

Estimate the sum of 44 + 27.
Find the nearest ten for each number.

40 41 42 43 **44** 45 46 47 48 49 **50**

The nearest ten for 44 is __40__.

20 21 22 23 24 25 26 **27** 28 29 **30**

The nearest ten for 27 is __30__.

__40__ + __30__ = __70__   An estimate of the sum is __70__.

Estimate the sum.

1. Estimate the sum of 23 + 31.

20 21 22 **23** 24 25 26 27 28 29 **30**

The nearest ten for 23 is __20__.

30 31 32 33 34 35 36 37 38 39 **40**

The nearest ten for 31 is __30__.

__20__ + __30__ = __50__   An estimate of the sum is __50__.

Reteach   GRR2   Grade 2

---

*GR – Getting Ready Lessons and Resources (*www.thinkcentral.com*)

On Your Own

Find the nearest ten for each number.
Add the tens to estimate.

2. Estimate the sum of 13 + 28.

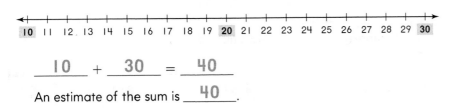

$$\underline{10} + \underline{30} = \underline{40}$$

An estimate of the sum is ____40____.

3. Estimate the sum of 31 + 22.

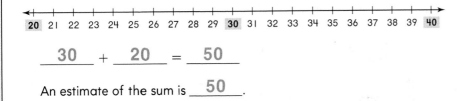

$$\underline{30} + \underline{20} = \underline{50}$$

An estimate of the sum is ____50____.

Problem Solving

Solve. Write or draw to explain.

4. Mark has 34 pennies. Emma has 47 pennies. Possible answer is given.
About how many pennies do they have altogether?

about ____80____ pennies

 TAKE HOME ACTIVITY • Ask your child to use the number line for Exercise 2 and describe how to estimate the sum of 27 + 21.

© Houghton Mifflin Harcourt Publishing Company

GR4 four

Use **Math Talk** to focus on children's understanding of how to find the nearest ten for a number.

▶ **On Your Own** • **Independent Practice**

If children answer Exercise 1 correctly, assign Exercises 2 and 3.

- **Look at your estimate for Exercise 3. How would your estimate have been different if you had used 40 + 30 to estimate the sum?** Possible answer: The estimate for the sum would have been 70 instead of 50.

- **Now find the actual sum of 31 + 22. Which estimate is closer to the actual sum?** The estimate of 50 is closer to the actual sum of 53.

▶ **Problem Solving**

For Exercise 4, make sure children understand that they are finding an estimate to answer the question.

UNLOCK THE PROBLEM In Exercise 4, children will estimate the sum of two 2-digit numbers without having a number line included with the problem. For children who are having difficulty, you may wish to draw a number line labeled from 30 to 50 on the board.

3 SUMMARIZE

Math Processes and Practices

Essential Question

How can you estimate the sum of two 2-digit numbers? Possible answer: I can find the ten that is nearest to each addend. Then I can add these tens to find an estimate of the sum.

Math Journal WRITE ▶ Math

Describe how to find an estimate for the sum of 47 + 12.

LESSON 3

Estimate Sums: 3-Digit Addition

LESSON AT A GLANCE

Lesson Objective
Estimate sums of 3-digit numbers.

Essential Question
How can you estimate the sum of two 3-digit numbers?

Materials
MathBoard

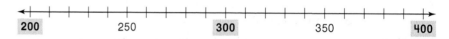

▸ Animated Math Models
*i*Tools: Number Line
HMH Mega Math

---

1 TEACH and TALK

▶ **Model and Draw** [Math Processes and Practices]

Discuss the example in the model with children.

- **Why is 200 written as the first addend in the addition sentence?** 200 is the nearest hundred to 189.

- **Why is 300 written as the second addend in the addition sentence?** 300 is the nearest hundred to 284.

- **Why is 200 + 300 a reasonable way to estimate the sum of 189 + 284?** Possible answer: 200 and 300 are the nearest hundreds to 189 and 284, so the sum of 200 and 300 will be close to the sum of 189 + 284.

This lesson builds on 3-digit addition skills taught in Chapter 6 and prepares children for rounding numbers and estimating multi-digit sums taught in Grade 3.

Name _____

Estimate Sums: 3-Digit Addition

Essential Question How can you estimate the sum of two 3-digit numbers?

Model and Draw

Estimate the sum of 189 + 284.
Find the nearest hundred for each number.

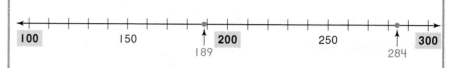

$\underline{200} + \underline{300} = \underline{500}$

An estimate of the sum is $\underline{500}$.

Share and Show [MATH BOARD]

Find the nearest hundred for each number.
Add the hundreds to estimate.

1. Estimate the sum of 229 + 386.

$\underline{200} + \underline{400} = \underline{600}$

An estimate of the sum is $\underline{600}$.

 Math Talk
How do you know which two hundreds a 3-digit number is between?

Possible answer: The hundreds digit tells me the hundred number before, and I can increase the hundreds digit by 1 to find the hundred number after.

Getting Ready for Grade 3   five **GR5**

GR: Practice, p. GRP3

Name _____   Lesson 3

Estimate Sums: 3-Digit Addition

Find the nearest hundred for each number.
Add the hundreds to estimate.

1. Estimate the sum of 332 + 459.

(number line: 300 350 400 450 500)

$\underline{300} + \underline{500} = \underline{800}$
An estimate of the sum is $\underline{800}$.

2. Estimate the sum of 295 + 198.

(number line: 100 150 200 250 300)

$\underline{300} + \underline{200} = \underline{500}$
An estimate of the sum is $\underline{500}$.

Problem Solving

Solve. Write or draw to explain.   Possible answer is given.

3. Anja collected shells at the beach. She has 377 shells in a box and 219 shells in a pail. Estimate the number of shells Anja has in all.

about $\underline{600}$ shells

Getting Ready for Grade 3   GRP3

GR: Reteach, p. GRR3

Name _____   Lesson 3 Reteach

Estimate Sums: 3-Digit Addition

Estimate the sum of 356 + 425.
Find the nearest hundred for each number.

(number line: 300 310 320 330 340 350 360 370 380 390 400, 356)

The nearest hundred for 356 is $\underline{400}$.

(number line: 400 410 420 430 440 450 460 470 480 490 500, 425)

The nearest hundred for 425 is $\underline{400}$.

$\underline{400} + \underline{400} = \underline{800}$ An estimate of the sum is $\underline{800}$.

Estimate the sum.

1. Estimate the sum of 265 + 436.

(number line: 200 210 220 230 240 250 260 270 280 290 300)

The nearest hundred for 265 is $\underline{300}$.

(number line: 400 410 420 430 440 450 460 470 480 490 500)

The nearest hundred for 436 is $\underline{400}$.

$\underline{300} + \underline{400} = \underline{700}$ An estimate of the sum is $\underline{700}$.

Reteach   GRR3   Grade 2

***GR** – Getting Ready Lessons and Resources (www.thinkcentral.com)

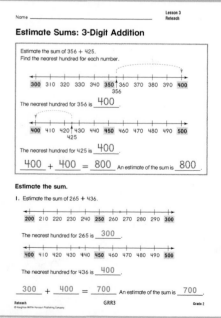

On Your Own

Find the nearest hundred for each number.
Add the hundreds to estimate.

2. Estimate the sum of 324 + 218.

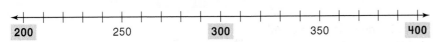

__300__ + __200__ = __500__

An estimate of the sum is __500__.

3. Estimate the sum of 468 + 439.

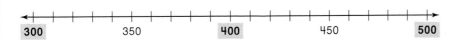

__500__ + __400__ = __900__

An estimate of the sum is __900__.

Problem Solving

Solve. Write or draw to explain.

4. There are 375 yellow fish and 283 blue fish   Possible answer is given.
swimming around a coral reef. About
how many fish are there altogether?

about __700__ fish

 TAKE HOME ACTIVITY • Ask your child to use the number line for
Exercise 2 and describe how to estimate the sum of 215 + 398.

GR6 six

© Houghton Mifflin Harcourt Publishing Company

2 PRACTICE

▶ **Share and Show** • **Guided Practice**

- **In Exercise 1, what did you do to estimate the sum?** Possible answer: I used the number line to find the nearest hundred for 229 and for 386. Then I found the sum of 200 and 400 to find an estimate for the sum of 229 and 386.

▶ **On Your Own** • **Independent Practice**

If children answer Exercise 1 correctly, assign Exercises 2 and 3.

- **Look at your estimate in Exercise 3. How would your estimate have been different if you had used 400 + 400 to estimate the sum?** Possible answer: The estimate for the sum would have been 800 instead of 900.

- **Without finding the actual sum, which estimate do you think will be closer to the actual sum? Explain.** Possible answer: I think the actual sum will be closer to 900, because both addends have several tens, so the actual sum will be much greater than 800.

▶ **Problem Solving**

For Exercise 4, make sure that children understand that they are finding an estimate to answer the question.

UNLOCK THE PROBLEM In Exercise 4, if children are having difficulty, you may wish to point out that they can use the number line in Exercise 2 as a tool for estimating the sum of the two numbers.

3 SUMMARIZE

Math Processes and Practices

Essential Question

How can you estimate the sum of two 3-digit numbers? Possible answer: I can find the hundred that is nearest to each addend. Then I can add these hundreds to find an estimate of the sum.

Math Journal  Math

Describe how to find an estimate for the sum of 261 + 375.

LESSON 4

Estimate Differences: 2-Digit Subtraction

LESSON AT A GLANCE

Lesson Objective
Estimate differences of 2-digit numbers.

Essential Question
How can you estimate the difference of two 2-digit numbers?

Materials
MathBoard

GO DIGITAL
iT *i*Tools: Base-Ten Blocks
MM HMH Mega Math

1 TEACH and TALK GO DIGITAL • Animated Math Models

▶ Model and Draw   Math Processes and Practices

As you work through the model, remind children that an estimate tells *about* how many.

- **Why does an arrow point from 48 to 50?** 50 is the nearest ten to 48. **Why does an arrow point from 62 to 60?** 60 is the nearest ten to 62.

- **Why are the arrow jumps on the number line pointing in different directions?** Possible answer: The arrow jumps are in different directions because the nearest ten to 48 is greater than 48 and the nearest ten to 62 is less than 62.

2 PRACTICE MATH BOARD

▶ Share and Show • Guided Practice

- **For Exercise 1, what will you do first to estimate the difference?** Possible answer: I will put dots on the number line for 42 and 29, and then find the nearest ten for each number.

PG56   Planning Guide

This lesson builds on 2-digit subtraction skills taught in Chapter 5 and prepares children for rounding numbers and estimating multi-digit differences taught in Grade 3.

Name _____

Estimate Differences: 2-Digit Subtraction

Essential Question How can you estimate the difference of two 2-digit numbers?

Model and Draw

Estimate the difference of 62 − 48.
Find the nearest ten for each number.

$$\underline{\quad 60 \quad} - \underline{\quad 50 \quad} = \underline{\quad 10 \quad}$$

An estimate of the difference is ___10___.

Share and Show MATH BOARD

Find the nearest ten for each number.
Subtract the tens to estimate.

1. Estimate the difference of 42 − 29.

$$\underline{\quad 40 \quad} - \underline{\quad 30 \quad} = \underline{\quad 10 \quad}$$

An estimate of the difference is ___10___.

Possible answer: The tens digit tells me the tens number before, and I can increase the tens digit by 1 to find the tens number after.

Math Talk   How do you know which two tens a number is between?

Getting Ready for Grade 3

seven **GR7**

GR: Practice, p. GRP4

Name _____   Lesson 4

Estimate Differences: 2-Digit Subtraction

Find the nearest ten for each number.
Subtract the tens to estimate.

1. Estimate the difference of 48 − 21.

$$\underline{\quad 50 \quad} - \underline{\quad 20 \quad} = \underline{\quad 30 \quad}$$

An estimate of the difference is ___30___.

2. Estimate the difference of 51 − 38.

$$\underline{\quad 50 \quad} - \underline{\quad 40 \quad} = \underline{\quad 10 \quad}$$

An estimate of the difference is ___10___.

Problem Solving

Solve. Write or draw to explain.

3. Hannah's class collected 37 bottles and 16 cans to recycle. About how many more bottles than cans did the class collect?   Possible answer is given.

about ___20___ more bottles

Getting Ready for Grade 3   GRP4

GR: Reteach, p. GRR4

Name _____   Lesson 4 Reteach

Estimate Differences: 2-Digit Subtraction

Estimate the difference of 41 − 29.
Find the nearest ten for each number.

The nearest ten for 41 is ___40___.

The nearest ten for 29 is ___30___.

$$\underline{\quad 40 \quad} - \underline{\quad 30 \quad} = \underline{\quad 10 \quad}$$ An estimate of the difference is ___10___.

Estimate the difference.

1. Estimate the difference of 77 − 36.

The nearest ten for 77 is ___80___.

The nearest ten for 36 is ___40___.

$$\underline{\quad 80 \quad} - \underline{\quad 40 \quad} = \underline{\quad 40 \quad}$$ An estimate of the difference is ___40___.

Reteach   GRR4   Grade 2

*****GR – Getting Ready Lessons and Resources (www.thinkcentral.com)**

On Your Own

Find the nearest ten for each number.
Subtract the tens to estimate.

2. Estimate the difference of 51 − 39.

$$\underline{50} - \underline{40} = \underline{10}$$

An estimate of the difference is ___10___.

3. Estimate the difference of 79 − 56.

$$\underline{80} - \underline{60} = \underline{20}$$

An estimate of the difference is ___20___.

Problem Solving

Solve. Write or draw to explain.

4. A farmer has 91 cows. 58 of the cows   Possible answer is given.
are in the barn. About how many of the
cows are not in the barn?

about ___30___ cows

 TAKE HOME ACTIVITY • Ask your child to use the number line for Exercise 2 and describe how to estimate the difference of 57 − 41.

GR8 eight

© Houghton Mifflin Harcourt Publishing Company

Use Math Talk to focus on children's understanding of which two tens a 2-digit number is between.

▶ **On Your Own** • Independent Practice

If children answer Exercise 1 correctly, assign Exercises 2 and 3.

Discuss with children that sometimes an estimate using this method may not result in the closest tens number to the actual difference. For example, using this method, the estimate for the difference of 54 − 37 is 10, but the actual difference (17) is closer to 20. Emphasize that estimation is used for a measure of reasonableness, rather than precision.

▶ **Problem Solving**

For Exercise 4, make sure children understand that they are finding an estimate to answer the question.

UNLOCK THE PROBLEM In Exercise 4, children will estimate a difference without having a number line included with the problem. For children who are having difficulty, have them work in pairs to brainstorm strategies for solving the problem.

3 SUMMARIZE

Math Processes and Practices

Essential Question

How can you estimate the difference of two 2-digit numbers? Possible answer: I can find the ten that is nearest to each number. Then I can subtract these tens to find an estimate of the difference.

Math Journal Math

Describe how to find an estimate for the difference of 61 − 23.

Estimate Differences: 3-Digit Subtraction

LESSON AT A GLANCE

Lesson Objective
Estimate differences of 3-digit numbers.

Essential Question
How can you estimate the difference of two 3-digit numbers?

Materials
MathBoard

GO DIGITAL

- ☑ Animated Math Models
- *iT* iTools: Number Line
- 𝖬𝖬 HMH Mega Math

1 TEACH and TALK
GO DIGITAL • Animated Math Models

▶ **Model and Draw**
Math Processes and Practices

Direct children's attention to the midpoints between each pair of hundreds on the number line: 250 and 350. Discuss how marking a point for a number before or after these midpoints helps them to know which is the nearest hundred. Then ask:

- **Why is finding the difference of 400 − 300 a reasonable way to estimate the difference of 382 − 265?** Possible answer: 400 and 300 are the nearest hundreds to 382 and 265, so the difference of 400 − 300 will be close to the difference of 382 − 265.

This lesson builds on 3-digit subtraction skills taught in Chapter 6 and prepares children for rounding numbers and estimating multi-digit differences taught in Grade 3.

Name _____

Estimate Differences: 3-Digit Subtraction

Essential Question How can you estimate the difference of two 3-digit numbers?

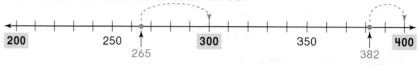
Model and Draw

Estimate the difference of 382 − 265.
Find the nearest hundred for each number.

A number line labeled 200, 250, 300, 350, 400 with points marked at 265 and 382.

$\underline{400} - \underline{300} = \underline{100}$

An estimate of the difference is ____100____.

Share and Show
MATH BOARD

Find the nearest hundred for each number.
Subtract the hundreds to estimate.

I. Estimate the difference of 674 − 590.

A number line labeled 500, 550, 600, 650, 700.

$\underline{700} - \underline{600} = \underline{100}$

An estimate of the difference is ____100____.

Possible answer: 674 is between 600 and 700. Looking at the number line, I can see that it is nearer to 700 than to 600.

Math Talk How did you know which hundred is nearest to 674?

Getting Ready for Grade 3

nine **GR9**

© Houghton Mifflin Harcourt Publishing Company

GR: Practice, p. GRP5

Name _____   Lesson 5
Estimate Differences: 3-Digit Subtraction

Find the nearest hundred for each number.
Subtract the hundreds to estimate.

I. Estimate the difference of 386 − 235.

A number line labeled 200, 250, 300, 350, 400.

$\underline{400} - \underline{200} = \underline{200}$

An estimate of the difference is ____200____.

2. Estimate the difference of 790 − 674.

A number line labeled 600, 650, 700, 750, 800.

$\underline{800} - \underline{700} = \underline{100}$

An estimate of the difference is ____100____.

Problem Solving

Solve. Write or draw to explain.

3. Max wants to have 425 baseball cards. He has 318 baseball cards right now. About how many more cards does he need to get?
Possible answer is given.

about ____100____ more cards

Getting Ready for Grade 3   GRP5

GR: Reteach, p. GRR5

Name _____   Lesson 5 Reteach
Estimate Differences: 3-Digit Subtraction

Estimate the difference of 634 − 436.
Find the nearest hundred for each number.

A number line labeled 600 610 620 630 640 650 660 670 680 690 700.

The nearest hundred for 634 is ____600____.

A number line labeled 400 410 420 430 440 450 460 470 480 490 500.

The nearest hundred for 436 is ____400____.

$\underline{600} - \underline{400} = \underline{200}$ An estimate of the difference is ____200____.

Estimate the difference.

I. Estimate the difference of 514 − 195.

A number line labeled 500 510 520 530 540 550 560 570 580 590 600.

The nearest hundred for 514 is ____500____.

A number line labeled 100 110 120 130 140 150 160 170 180 190 200.

The nearest hundred for 195 is ____200____.

$\underline{500} - \underline{200} = \underline{300}$ An estimate of the difference is ____300____.

Reteach   GRR5   Grade 2
© Houghton Mifflin Harcourt Publishing Company

---

*GR – Getting Ready Lessons and Resources (*www.thinkcentral.com*)

On Your Own

Find the nearest hundred for each number.
Subtract the hundreds to estimate.

2. Estimate the difference of 791 − 612.

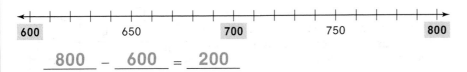

___800___ − ___600___ = ___200___

An estimate of the difference is ___200___ .

3. Estimate the difference of 487 − 309.

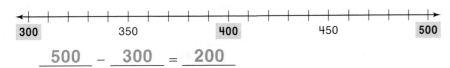

___500___ − ___300___ = ___200___

An estimate of the difference is ___200___ .

Problem Solving

Solve. Write or draw to explain.

4. A mail carrier had 819 letters to deliver.
Then she delivered 687 letters. About how
many letters does she still have to deliver?

Possible answer is given.

about ___100___ letters

TAKE HOME ACTIVITY • Ask your child to use the number line for Exercise 2
and describe how to estimate the difference of 786 − 611.

GR10 ten

© Houghton Mifflin Harcourt Publishing Company

---

② PRACTICE

▶ Share and Show • Guided Practice

• **In Exercise 1, the nearest hundred to 590
is 600. What are two other numbers for
which the nearest hundred is 600?** Check
children's answers for understanding. Possible
answer: 572 and 619

Use Math Talk to focus on children's
understanding of how to find the hundreds
number that is nearest to a number.

▶ On Your Own • Independent Practice

If children answer Exercise 1 correctly, assign
Exercises 2 and 3. After children complete
these exercises, you may wish to ask:

• **Look at Exercise 2. Do the tens digits
in 791 and 612 help you to know
which is the nearest hundred for each
number? Explain.** Check children's answers for
understanding.

▶ Problem Solving

For Exercise 4, make sure children
understand that they are finding an
estimate to answer the question.

UNLOCK THE PROBLEM In Exercise 4, children
will estimate a difference without having
a number line included with the problem.
You may wish to have children work in small
groups and solve the problem together.

③ SUMMARIZE

Math Processes and Practices

Essential Question

**How can you estimate the difference of two
3-digit numbers?** Possible answer: I can find the
hundred that is nearest to each number. Then I can
subtract these hundreds to find an estimate of the
difference.

Math Journal · WRITE Math

Suppose you are estimating the difference
of 527 − 183. Would you use 600 − 100?
Explain.

LESSON 6

Order 3-Digit Numbers

LESSON AT A GLANCE

Lesson Objective
Order three 3-digit numbers from least to greatest.

Essential Question
How does place value help you order 3-digit numbers?

Materials
MathBoard

GO DIGITAL

☑ Animated Math Models
MM HMH Mega Math

---

1 TEACH and TALK GO DIGITAL • Animated Math Models

▶ **Model and Draw** Math Processes and Practices

Direct children's attention to the example in the model. Discuss how children will compare the numbers so that they can then write them in order from least to greatest.

- **What do you find when you compare the hundreds, and how does this help you order the 3 numbers?** 418 has the most hundreds. So I can write 418 as the greatest number. Then I have only 2 numbers left to compare.

- **Since 249 and 205 have the same number of hundreds, what do you compare next?** Possible answer: I compare the tens in the numbers next. 0 tens is less than 4 tens, so 205 is less than 249.

You may wish to discuss with children how ordering these three numbers combines the two comparison statements 205 < 249 and 249 < 418.

PG60 Planning Guide

Name _____

Order 3-Digit Numbers

Essential Question: How does place value help you order 3-digit numbers?

This lesson builds on comparing two 3-digit numbers taught in Chapter 2 and prepares children for comparing and ordering fractions taught in Grade 3.

Model and Draw

You can order 249, 418, and 205 from least to greatest. First, compare the **hundreds**. Next, compare the tens and then the ones, if needed.

Hundreds	Tens	Ones
2	4	9
4	1	8
2	0	5

I compare the hundreds. 249 and 205 are both less than 418.

Which is less, 249 or 205? I compare the tens. 205 is less than 249, so 205 is the least.

$$\underline{205} < \underline{249} < \underline{418}$$
least   greatest

Share and Show MATH BOARD

Write the numbers in order from least to greatest.

1.
```
6 7 2
5 1 5
5 3 2
```
$\underline{515} < \underline{532} < \underline{672}$

2.
```
7 8 7
6 8 3
5 6 4
```
$\underline{564} < \underline{683} < \underline{787}$

Possible answer: No. If you already know the order from comparing hundreds and tens, there's no reason to compare the ones.

Math Talk Do you always need to compare the ones digits when you order numbers? Explain.

Getting Ready for Grade 3   eleven **GR11**

© Houghton Mifflin Harcourt Publishing Company

GR: Practice, p. GRP6

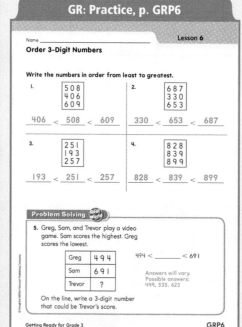

GR: Reteach, p. GRR6

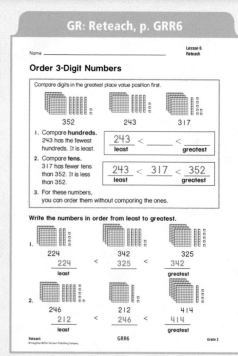

*GR – Getting Ready Lessons and Resources (www.thinkcentral.com)

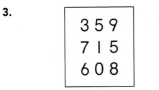

On Your Own

Write the numbers in order from least to greatest.

3.

```
3 5 9
7 1 5
6 0 8
```

359 < 608 < 715

4.

```
9 5 9
9 1 5
9 0 8
```

908 < 915 < 959

5.

```
3 4 3
3 4 1
3 4 8
```

341 < 343 < 348

6.

```
1 6 5
7 4 6
7 6 4
```

165 < 746 < 764

Problem Solving

7. Brenda, Jean, and Pam play a video game. Brenda scores the highest. Jean scores the lowest.

Brenda	8 6 3
Jean	7 6 7
Pam	?

On the line, write a 3-digit number that could be Pam's score.

767 < ___ < 863

Answers will vary.
Possible answers: 852, 800, 798, 777

 TAKE HOME ACTIVITY • Write three 3-digit numbers. Have your child tell you how to order the numbers from least to greatest.

GR12 twelve

© Houghton Mifflin Harcourt Publishing Company

Getting Ready Lessons and Resources, pp. GR13–GR14   ✓ Checkpoint

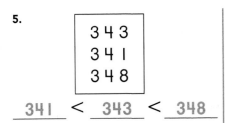

Name _____

✓ Checkpoint

Concepts and Skills

1. Write the missing sums in the addition table.

Find the nearest ten.

2. Estimate the sum of 24 and 36.

20 + 40 = 60
An estimate of the sum is 60.

Find the nearest hundred.

3. Estimate the sum of 285 and 122.

300 + 100 = 400
An estimate of the sum is 400.

Getting Ready for Grade 3   thirteen **GR13**

Find the nearest ten.

4. Estimate the difference of 72 − 59.

70 − 60 = 10
An estimate of the difference is 10.

Find the nearest hundred.

5. Estimate the difference of 792 and 619.

800 − 600 = 200
An estimate of the difference is 200.

6. Which of the following numbers will make this true?

350 < 413 < _____.

○ 403
○ 398
◉ 430
○ 331

GR14 fourteen

---

2 PRACTICE

▶ **Share and Show** • Guided Practice

- **In Exercise 2, what do you know after comparing the hundreds digits?** Possible answer: Since all three hundreds digits are different, I can order the numbers from least to greatest just by using their hundreds digits. Since 5 < 6 < 7, I know that 564 < 683 < 787.

▶ **On Your Own** • Independent Practice

If children complete Exercises 1–2 correctly, assign Exercises 3–6. Remind children that they are ordering the numbers from least to greatest.

- **How do you decide which number is least?** Possible answer: I compare hundreds first. Then I compare tens if the hundreds are the same. Then I compare the ones if needed.

- **Where do you write the number that is the least of the three numbers?** Possible answer: I write it on the first blank on the left.

▶ **Problem Solving**

UNLOCK THE PROBLEM Read aloud the problem in Exercise 7. The problem presents an everyday situation that involves ordering numbers.

- **How can you choose a number that is greater than 767 but is less than 863?** Check children's answers for understanding.

3 SUMMARIZE

Math Processes and Practices

Essential Question

How does place value help you order 3-digit numbers? Possible answer: When you order numbers, you look at the digits in the greatest place value position first and compare them. If these digits are the same, then you compare digits in the next greatest place value position.

Math Journal   WRITE Math

Make a list of three different 3-digit numbers. Then write them in order from least to greatest.

LESSON **7**

Equal Groups of 2

LESSON AT A GLANCE

Lesson Objective
Find the total number of objects in equal groups of 2.

Essential Question
How can you find the total number in equal groups of 2?

Materials
MathBoard

GO DIGITAL iT *i*Tools: Counters

---

1 TEACH and TALK **GO DIGITAL** · Animated Math Models

▶ Model and Draw [Math Processes and Practices]

Point out the counters at the top of the page. Discuss how the 3 groups of 2 counters are used to stand for the 3 fishbowls with 2 goldfish in each fishbowl. Then ask:

- **How can you find how many counters there are in all?** Possible answers: I can add 2 + 2 + 2. I can count by twos: 2, 4, 6.

- **Can counting by twos be a way to add equal groups of two? Explain.** Yes; Possible explanation: As you count on by twos, you are finding a total amount, which is what you do when you add equal groups together.

---

2 PRACTICE **MATH BOARD**

▶ Share and Show · Guided Practice

- **Look at Exercise 3. Are the groups equal?** yes **How do you know?** Possible answer: Each group has the same number of counters: 2 counters.

PG62 Planning Guide

This lesson builds on using repeated addition to find the total number of objects in arrays taught in Chapter 3 and prepares children for describing the total number of objects in equal groups as a product, taught in Grade 3.

Name _____

Equal Groups of 2

Essential Question: How can you find the total number in equal groups of 2?

The pet store has 3 fishbowls in the window. There are 2 goldfish in each bowl. How many goldfish are there in all?

Make 3 groups of 2 counters.

I can count the equal groups by twos—2, 4, 6—to find how many in all.

___3___ groups of ___2___ is ___6___ in all.

Share and Show **MATH BOARD**

Complete the sentence to show how many in all.

1.

___4___ groups of ___2___ is ___8___ in all.

2.

___2___ groups of ___2___ is ___4___ in all.

3.

___3___ groups of ___2___ is ___6___ in all.

 Math Talk How can you use counters to find 2 + 2 + 2 + 2 + 2?

Possible answer: Show 5 groups of counters with 2 counters in each group. Then count the counters by twos to find how many in all.

Getting Ready for Grade 3

fifteen **GR15**

GR: Practice, p. GRP7

Name _____ Lesson 7
Equal Groups of 2

Complete the sentence to show how many in all.

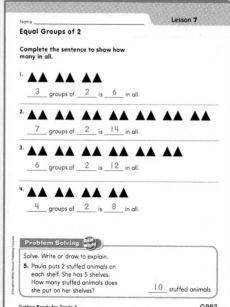

GR: Reteach, p. GRR7

Name _____ Lesson 7 Reteach
Equal Groups of 2

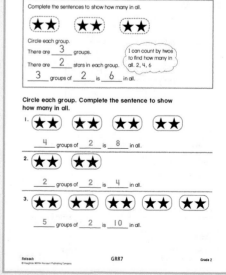

---

*GR – Getting Ready Lessons and Resources (*www.thinkcentral.com*)

Complete the sentence to show how many in all.

4.

_8_ groups of _2_ is _16_ in all.

5.

_5_ groups of _2_ is _10_ in all.

6.

_7_ groups of _2_ is _14_ in all.

7.

_6_ groups of _2_ is _12_ in all.

 Problem Solving

Solve. Write or draw to explain.

8. Coach Baker keeps 2 basketballs in each bin. There are 5 bins. How many basketballs are stored in the bins?

_10_ basketballs

© Houghton Mifflin Harcourt Publishing Company

 TAKE HOME ACTIVITY • Have your child draw groups of two Xs and tell you how to find how many there are in all.

GR16 sixteen

▶ **On Your Own** • Independent Practice
If children completed Exercises 1–3 correctly, assign Exercises 4–7.

• **Why do you count by twos instead of one by one?** Possible answer: When you are adding equal groups of 2, it is faster to count by twos.

▶ **Problem Solving**

UNLOCK THE PROBLEM Read the word problem in Exercise 8 together. Discuss the problem as a class.

• **What do you know?** There are 2 basketballs in each bin. There are 5 bins.

• **How can you use groups of 2 to describe what you know?** There are 5 groups of 2.

• **What will you do to solve this problem?** Possible answer: I will count by twos to find how many basketballs are stored in the 5 bins.

3 SUMMARIZE

Math Processes and Practices

Essential Question

How can you find the total number in equal groups of 2? Possible answer: You can count by twos to find how many in all.

Math Journal

Write a word problem about 7 groups of 2. Draw to show the problem and explain how to solve it.

This lesson builds on using repeated addition to find the total number of objects in arrays taught in Chapter 3 and prepares children for describing the number of objects in equal groups as a product, taught in Grade 3.

LESSON 8

Equal Groups of 5

LESSON AT A GLANCE

Lesson Objective
Find the total number of objects in equal groups of 5.

Essential Question
How can you find the total number in equal groups of 5?

Materials
MathBoard

 *i*Tools: Counters

---

1 TEACH and TALK • Animated Math Models

▶ Model and Draw · Math Processes and Practices

Review with children how they used counting by twos in the previous lesson to find the total number for equal groups of two. Then discuss the picture shown next to the problem.

- **Are the 3 groups of cubes equal?** yes **How many cubes are in each group?** 5 cubes
- **How can you find how many cubes there are in all?** Possible answers: You can add 5 + 5 + 5. You can count by fives.

2 PRACTICE

▶ Share and Show • Guided Practice

- **Look at the picture of cubes in Exercise 1. How is this picture like the picture in the example at the top of the page?** The picture in Exercise 1 shows equal groups of 5 cubes, like the picture in the example shows. **How are the pictures of cubes different?** The number of groups is different.

PG64 Planning Guide

Name _____

Equal Groups of 5

Essential Question: How can you find the total number in equal groups of 5?

Model and Draw

Luke made 3 cube trains. He connected 5 cubes in each train. How many cubes did he use in all?

Make 3 groups of 5 cubes.

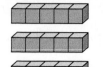

I can count the equal groups by fives—5, 10, 15—to find how many in all.

__3__ groups of __5__ is __15__ in all.

Share and Show · MATH BOARD

Complete the sentence to show how many in all.

1.

__2__ groups of __5__ is __10__ in all.

2.

__4__ groups of __5__ is __20__ in all.

3.
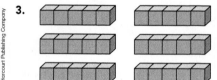

__6__ groups of __5__ is __30__ in all.

 Math Talk How can you use addition to find how many in all in Exercise 2? Possible answer: You could add 5 + 5 + 5 + 5.

Getting Ready for Grade 3   seventeen **GR17**

© Houghton Mifflin Harcourt Publishing Company

GR: Practice, p. GRP8

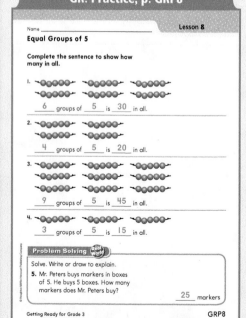

GR: Reteach, p. GRR8

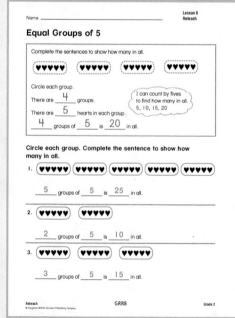

*GR – Getting Ready Lessons and Resources (*www.thinkcentral.com*)

On Your Own

Complete the sentences to show how many in all.

4.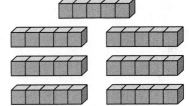

_7_ groups of _5_ is _35_ in all.

5.

_5_ groups of _5_ is _25_ in all.

6.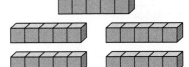

_8_ groups of _5_ is _40_ in all.

Problem Solving Real World

Solve. Write or draw to explain.

7. Gina fills 6 pages of her photo album. She puts 5 photos on each page. How many photos does Gina put in her album?

_30_ photos

 TAKE HOME ACTIVITY • Place your hands next to your child's hands. Ask how many groups of 5 fingers. Have your child tell you how to find how many in all. How many fingers in all?

GRI8 eighteen

© Houghton Mifflin Harcourt Publishing Company

▶ **On Your Own** • Independent Practice

If children completed Exercises 1–3 correctly, have them continue with Exercises 4–6.

• **Look at Exercise 6. What addition sentence could you write for the picture of equal groups of 5?** Possible answer: 5 + 5 + 5 + 5 +5 + 5 + 5 + 5 = 40.

▶ **Problem Solving**

UNLOCK THE PROBLEM Discuss the word problem in Exercise 7.

• **What do you know?** Gina fills 6 pages. She puts 5 photos on each page.

• **Describe a drawing that you could use to show the problem.** Possible answer: A drawing of 6 groups of 5 squares could be used to show the problem.

3 SUMMARIZE

Math Processes and Practices

Essential Question

How can you find the total number in equal groups of 5? Possible answer: You can add fives or count by fives to find how many in all.

Math Journal WRITE Math

Draw a picture of several equal groups of 5 objects. Describe how to find the total number of objects there are in all.

LESSON 9

Equal Groups of 10

LESSON AT A GLANCE

Lesson Objective
Find the total number of objects in equal groups of 10.

Essential Question
How can you find the total number in equal groups of 10?

Materials
MathBoard

*i*Tools: Number Line

HMH Mega Math

1 TEACH and TALK
• Animated Math Models

▶ Model and Draw Math Processes and Practices

Read the problem in the example with children. Discuss how the 4 groups of 10 cubes are used to stand for the 4 packs with 10 juice boxes in each pack. Then ask:

- **How can you find how many cubes there are in all?** Possible answers: You can add 10 + 10 + 10 + 10. You can count by tens: 10, 20, 30, 40.

2 PRACTICE

▶ Share and Show • Guided Practice

After children complete Exercises 1–3, ask the following question:

- **In Exercises 1–3, do you see a pattern in the numbers of groups and the numbers for the totals? Explain.** Possible answer: Yes; The number of groups is the same as the tens digit in the number for the total.

This lesson builds on using repeated addition to find the total number of objects in arrays taught in Chapter 3 and prepares children for describing the total number of objects in equal groups as a product, taught in Grade 3.

Name _____

Equal Groups of 10

Essential Question: How can you find the total number in equal groups of 10?

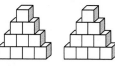

Model and Draw

There are 4 packs of juice. Each pack has 10 juice boxes. How many juice boxes are there in all?

Make 4 groups of 10 cubes.

__4__ groups of __10__ is __40__ in all.

> I can count the equal groups by tens—10, 20, 30, 40—to find how many in all.

Share and Show
MATH BOARD

Complete the sentence to show how many in all.

1.

__3__ groups of __10__ is __30__ in all.

2.

__2__ groups of __10__ is __20__ in all.

3.

__6__ groups of __10__ is __60__ in all.

 Math Talk How many groups of ten are in 70? Possible answer: Explain. There are 7 groups of ten because 70 is 7 tens and 0 ones.

Getting Ready for Grade 3

nineteen **GR19**

GR: Practice, p. GRP9

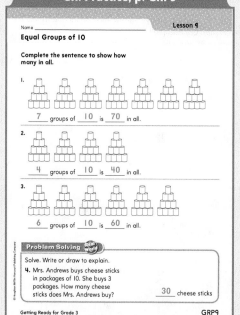

Name _____ Lesson 9

Equal Groups of 10

Complete the sentence to show how many in all.

1.
__7__ groups of __10__ is __70__ in all.

2.
__4__ groups of __10__ is __40__ in all.

3.
__6__ groups of __10__ is __60__ in all.

Problem Solving

Solve. Write or draw to explain.

4. Mrs. Andrews buys cheese sticks in packages of 10. She buys 3 packages. How many cheese sticks does Mrs. Andrews buy? __30__ cheese sticks

Getting Ready for Grade 3 GRP9

GR: Reteach, p. GRR9

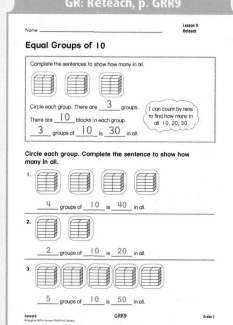

Name _____ Lesson 9 Reteach

Equal Groups of 10

Complete the sentences to show how many in all.

Circle each group. There are __3__ groups.
There are __10__ blocks in each group.
__3__ groups of __10__ is __30__ in all.

> I can count by tens to find how many in all. 10, 20, 30

Circle each group. Complete the sentence to show how many in all.

1.
__4__ groups of __10__ is __40__ in all.

2.
__2__ groups of __10__ is __20__ in all.

3.
__5__ groups of __10__ is __50__ in all.

Reteach GRR9 Grade 2

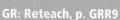 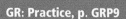

*GR – Getting Ready Lessons and Resources (*www.thinkcentral.com*)

On Your Own

Complete the sentence to show how many in all.

4.

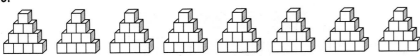

_7_ groups of _10_ is _70_ in all.

5.

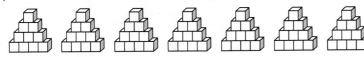

_8_ groups of _10_ is _80_ in all.

6.

_5_ groups of _10_ is _50_ in all.

Problem Solving

Solve. Write or draw to explain.

7. To count his pennies, Travis puts 10 pennies in a stack. He makes 4 stacks. How many pennies does Travis have?

_40_ pennies

 TAKE HOME ACTIVITY • Give your child 30 pieces of macaroni or other small objects. Have your child make groups of 10. Ask how many groups there are. Ask your child to tell you how to find how many in all. How many pieces in all?

© Houghton Mifflin Harcourt Publishing Company

GR20 twenty

On Your Own • Independent Practice

If children answer Exercises 1–3 correctly, assign Exercises 4–6.

- **Look at Exercise 4. Is counting each cube by ones or counting the groups of cubes by tens a better way to find the total number of cubes? Explain.** Answers may vary. Discuss how counting by tens can be done faster than counting by ones.

Problem Solving

UNLOCK THE PROBLEM Have children read the word problem in Exercise 7. Children need to understand that the pennies are in equal groups.

- **How many stacks of 10 pennies does Travis make?** 4 stacks of 10 pennies
- **Describe a drawing that you could use to show the problem.** Possible answer: A drawing of 4 groups of 10 circles each could be used to show the problem.

3 SUMMARIZE

Math Processes and Practices

Essential Question

How can you find the total number in equal groups of 10? Possible answer: You can count by tens or add groups of 10 to find how many there are in all.

Math Journal  Math

Jenny puts 10 raisins on each cookie. Draw some of her cookies. Tell the number of groups of 10 raisins and how many raisins there are in all.

Hands On: Size of Shares

LESSON AT A GLANCE

Lesson Objective
Make equal groups and find the number in each group.

Essential Question
How can you place items in equal groups?

Vocabulary
divide

Materials
MathBoard, two-color counters

☑ Animated Math Models
iT iTools: Counters
MM HMH Mega Math

---

1 TEACH and TALK · Animated Math Models

▶ **Model and Draw** Math Processes and Practices

Materials two-color counters

Have children make a group of 12 counters. Read the problem. Then have children model the problem by placing the counters into equal groups of 2 counters as shown in the example. Finally, have children draw the equal groups on their MathBoards.

- **Why are there 6 groups in the model?** There are 6 rabbits and each group stands for 1 rabbit.

- **Why are there 2 counters in each group?** If you place 12 carrots into 6 equal groups, each group will have 2 carrots.

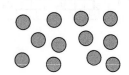

This lesson builds on the concept of equal groups presented in Chapter 3 and prepares children for the concept of division taught in Grade 3.

Name _____

Size of Shares

Essential Question How can you place items in equal groups?

Model and Draw

When you <u>divide</u>, you place items in equal groups. Joel has 12 carrots. There are 6 rabbits. Each rabbit gets the same number of carrots. How many carrots does each rabbit get?

Place 12 counters in 6 equal groups.

 counters in each group   So, each rabbit gets __2__ carrots.

Share and Show MATH BOARD

Use counters. Draw to show your work.
Write how many in each group.

1. Place 10 counters in 2 equal groups.

__5__ counters in each group

2. Place 6 counters in 3 equal groups.

Math Talk: Possible answer: I made 3 groups. I placed 1 counter in each group. I had 3 counters left. So, I placed 1 more counter in each group.

__2__ counters in each group

 Math Talk How did you know how many counters to place in each group for Exercise 2?

Getting Ready for Grade 3   twenty-one **GR21**

© Houghton Mifflin Harcourt Publishing Company

GR: Practice, p. GRP10

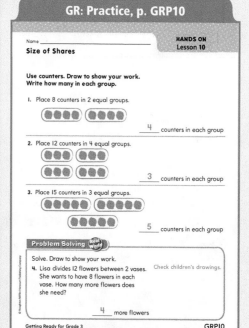

GR: Reteach, p. GRR10

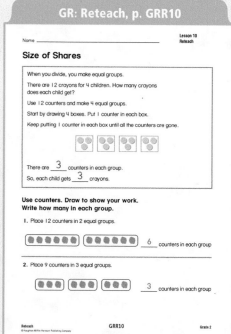

PG68 Planning Guide

*GR – Getting Ready Lessons and Resources (www.thinkcentral.com)

On Your Own

Use counters. Draw to show your work.
Write how many in each group.

3. Place 9 counters in 3 equal groups.

__3__ counters in each group

4. Place 12 counters in 2 equal groups.

__6__ counters in each group

5. Place 16 counters in 4 equal groups.

__4__ counters in each group

Problem Solving (Real World)

Solve. Draw to show your work.

Check children's drawings.

6. Mrs. Peters divides 6 orange slices between 2 plates. She wants to have 4 orange slices on each plate. How many more orange slices does she need?

__2__ more orange slices

 TAKE HOME ACTIVITY • Ask your child to place 15 pennies into 3 equal groups, and then tell how many pennies are in each group.

GR22 twenty-two

© Houghton Mifflin Harcourt Publishing Company

2 PRACTICE

▶ **Share and Show** • Guided Practice

For Exercise 1 have each child draw 2 loops on their MathBoards. Each loop should be large enough for children to place a few counters inside. Then have children move one counter at a time into each loop until they have placed all of the counters equally.

▶ **On Your Own** • Independent Practice

If children answer Exercises 1 and 2 correctly, assign Exercises 3–5. You may wish to have children share their drawings.

- **For Exercise 3, describe what you did with the 9 counters to solve the problem.** Check children's explanations.

- **In Exercise 5, how many counters would be in each group if you placed 16 counters in 2 equal groups?** 8 counters

▶ **Problem Solving**

UNLOCK THE PROBLEM Have children read the multistep problem in Exercise 6. You may wish to guide children's thinking by asking the following questions:

- **How many slices are on each plate when Mrs. Peters divides 6 orange slices between 2 plates?** 3 slices

- **How many total slices will she need if she wants to have 4 slices on each plate?** 8 slices

3 SUMMARIZE

Math Processes and Practices

Essential Question

How can you place items in equal groups?
Possible answer: I can draw a circle for each group. Then I can move one item at a time into each group until all of the items have been placed. I can count the items in each group to make sure each group has an equal number of items.

Math Journal WRITE Math

Draw and write to explain how to divide 12 counters into 3 equal groups.

LESSON 11

Hands On: Number of Equal Shares

LESSON AT A GLANCE

Lesson Objective
Make equal groups and find the number of groups.

Essential Question
How can you find the number of equal groups that items can be placed into?

Materials
MathBoard, two-color counters

- Animated Math Models
- iT iTools: Counters
- HMH Mega Math

1 TEACH and TALK 🔵 DIGITAL • Animated Math Models

▶ **Model and Draw** Math Processes and Practices

Materials two-color counters

Have children make a group of 12 counters. Read the problem with children. Then have children model the problem using their counters and placing them as shown in the example.

- **How many counters did you put in each group?** 3 counters **Why?** Each group of 3 counters stands for the 3 cookies that fill a snack bag.

- **Why did you make 4 groups?** If you put 3 cookies in each snack bag, 12 cookies will fill 4 bags.

This lesson builds on the concept of equal groups presented in Chapter 8 and prepares children for the concept of division taught in Grade 3.

Name _____

Lesson 11

Number of Equal Shares

Essential Question How can you find the number of equal groups that items can be placed into?

Model and Draw

There are 12 cookies. 3 cookies fill a snack bag. How many snack bags can be filled?

Place 12 counters in groups of 3.

4 groups

So, 4 snack bags can be filled.

Share and Show 🔲 MATH BOARD

Use counters. Draw to show your work. Write how many groups.

Math Talk: Possible answer: Begin with 12 counters. Keep making groups of 2 until you run out of counters. Count the groups you made.

1. Place 8 counters in groups of 4.

2 groups

2. Place 10 counters in groups of 2.

5 groups

Math Talk **Describe** how you could find the number of groups of 2 you could make with 12 counters.

Getting Ready for Grade 3

twenty-three **GR23**

GR: Practice, p. GRP11

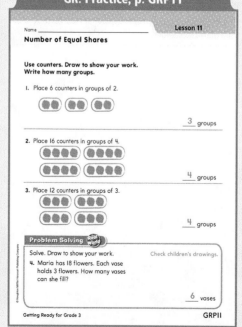

Name _____ Lesson 11
Number of Equal Shares

Use counters. Draw to show your work.
Write how many groups.

1. Place 6 counters in groups of 2.

3 groups

2. Place 16 counters in groups of 4.

4 groups

3. Place 12 counters in groups of 3.

4 groups

Problem Solving

Solve. Draw to show your work. Check children's drawings.

4. Maria has 18 flowers. Each vase holds 3 flowers. How many vases can she fill?

6 vases

Getting Ready for Grade 3   GRP11

GR: Reteach, p. GRR11

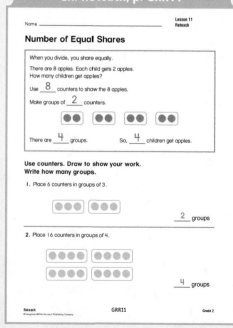

Name _____ Lesson 11
Reteach
Number of Equal Shares

When you divide, you share equally.
There are 8 apples. Each child gets 2 apples.
How many children get apples?

Use 8 counters to show the 8 apples.

Make groups of 2 counters.

There are 4 groups.   So, 4 children get apples.

Use counters. Draw to show your work.
Write how many groups.

1. Place 6 counters in groups of 3.

2 groups

2. Place 16 counters in groups of 4.

4 groups

Reteach   GRR11   Grade 2

PG70   Planning Guide

*GR – Getting Ready Lessons and Resources (*www.thinkcentral.com*)

On Your Own

Use counters. Draw to show your work.
Write how many groups.

3. Place 4 counters in groups of 2.

<u>2</u> groups

4. Place 12 counters in groups of 4.

<u>3</u> groups

5. Place 15 counters in groups of 3.

<u>5</u> groups

Problem Solving

Draw to show your work.
Check children's drawings.

6. Some children want to play a board game. There are 16 game pieces. Each player needs to have 4 pieces. How many children can play?

<u>4</u> children

 TAKE HOME ACTIVITY • Use small items such as pennies or cereal. Have your child find out how many groups of 5 are in 20.

© Houghton Mifflin Harcourt Publishing Company

GR24 twenty-four

---

(2) PRACTICE

▶ **Share and Show** • **Guided Practice**

For Exercise 1, tell children to place 4 counters in a group and continue making groups of 4 until all of the counters have been used.

Use Math Talk to focus on children's understanding of how to divide objects into equal groups to find the number of groups.

▶ **On Your Own** • **Independent Practice**

If children answer Exercises 1 and 2 correctly, assign Exercises 3–5. You may wish to have children share their drawings.

- **How many equal groups of 3 did you show for the 15 counters in Exercise 5?**
  5 equal groups of 3

▶ **Problem Solving**

UNLOCK THE PROBLEM For Exercise 6, children will solve a real-world problem involving equal groups. Unlike the previous exercises in this lesson, children will not use concrete materials before drawing a picture to solve this problem.

Ask volunteers to explain how they solved this problem. Encourage children to share their drawings.

(3) SUMMARIZE

Math Processes and Practices

Essential Question

How can you find the number of equal groups that items can be placed into? Possible answer: If I know how many items are in each group, then I can place the items into groups with that number until all the items are placed. Then I can count the number of equal groups.

Math Journal

Draw and write to explain how to place 8 counters into groups of 2 counters.

LESSON 12

Solve Problems with Equal Shares

LESSON AT A GLANCE

Lesson Objective
Solve problems that involve equal shares.

Essential Question
How can you solve word problems that involve equal shares?

Materials
MathBoard

GO DIGITAL
- Animated Math Models
- *i*Tools: Counters
- HMH Mega Math

1 TEACH and TALK
GO DIGITAL • Animated Math Models

▶ **Model and Draw** [Math Processes and Practices]

With children, read the problem in the model. Point out that this is a problem in which equal groups of objects are being counted to find a total amount. Discuss how the drawing is used to stand for the problem.

- **What does the drawing show?** 3 bags that each have 10 marbles in them

- **Are all the groups equal?** yes **How do you know?** Each bag has the same number of marbles in it: 10 marbles.

- **How many marbles are there in all?** 30 marbles **How do you know?** Check children's answers for understanding of how to find total amounts for equal groups.

This lesson builds on problems involving equal groups presented in Chapter 3 and prepares children for solving multiplication and division problems in Grade 3.

Name _____

Solve Problems with Equal Shares

Essential Question: How can you solve word problems that involve equal shares?

Model and Draw

You can draw a picture to help you solve problems with equal shares.

There are 10 marbles in each bag. How many marbles are in 3 bags?

10   10   10

__3__ groups of __10__ is __30__ in all.
There are __30__ marbles.

Share and Show   MATH BOARD

Solve. Draw or write to show what you did.

1. There are 5 oranges in each sack. How many oranges are in 4 sacks?

   Check children's drawings.

   __20__ oranges

2. Sandy can plant 2 seeds in a pot. How many pots will Sandy need in order to plant 6 seeds?

   Check children's drawings.

   __3__ pots

 Math Talk   Explain how you solved Exercise 2.   Possible answer: I kept drawing pots for 2 seeds until I got to a total of 6 seeds.

Getting Ready for Grade 3   twenty-five **GR25**

© Houghton Mifflin Harcourt Publishing Company

GR: Practice, p. GRP12

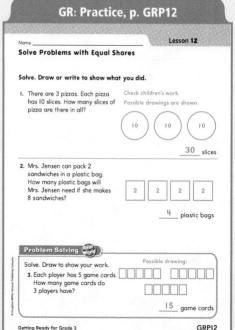

GR: Reteach, p. GRR12

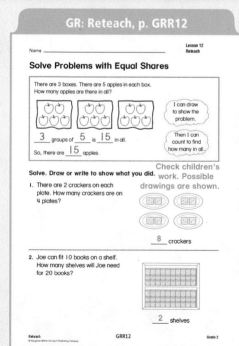

---

*GR – Getting Ready Lessons and Resources (*www.thinkcentral.com*)

On Your Own

Solve. Draw to show what you did.

3. Ben gives each friend 2 crackers. How many crackers does he need for 6 friends?

Check children's drawings.

_12_ crackers

4. Mrs. Green can pack 5 books in a box. How many boxes will she need in order to pack 15 books?

Check children's drawings.

_3_ boxes

Problem Solving

5. Franco used 12 connecting cubes to build towers. All the towers are the same height. Draw a picture to show the towers he could have built.

Check children's drawings.

© Houghton Mifflin Harcourt Publishing Company

TAKE HOME ACTIVITY • Ask your child to make up a word problem about 3 boxes of toys with 3 toys in each box. Have your child tell you how to solve the problem.

GR26 twenty-six

Getting Ready Lessons and Resources, pp. GR27–GR28   ✓ **Checkpoint**

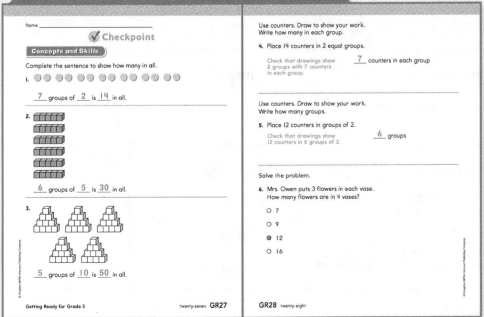

---

② PRACTICE

▶ Share and Show • Guided Practice

Have children solve Exercises 1 and 2. Then ask:

- **Did you solve these two problems in the same way? Explain.** Possible answer: No; for the first problem, I found the number of oranges in all. For the second problem, I divided the total number of seeds into equal groups to find how many groups of seeds there were.

▶ On Your Own • Independent Practice

If children answer Exercises 1–2 correctly, assign Exercises 3–4.

- **Read the problem in Exercise 4. What do you know?** 5 books fit in one box. There are 15 books in all. **What do you need to find?** the number of boxes that are needed

▶ Problem Solving

UNLOCK THE PROBLEM Have children read the problem in Exercise 5. You may wish to suggest that children first draw pictures on their MathBoards as they work to solve the problem. Then have children draw their solutions on the lesson page.

③ SUMMARIZE

Math Processes and Practices

Essential Question

How can you solve word problems that involve equal shares? Possible answer: You can draw equal groups to find how many there are in all. You can also draw to find the number of equal groups or to find how many there are in each of the equal groups.

Math Journal WRITE) Math

Write a problem about sharing 15 objects equally among 3 groups. Draw a picture and describe how to solve the problem.

Getting Ready for Grade 3
Test

LESSONS 1 TO 12

Summative Assessment

Use the **Getting Ready Test** to assess children's progress in Getting Ready for Grade 3 Lessons 1–12.

Getting Ready Tests are provided in multiple-choice and mixed-response format in the *Getting Ready Lessons and Resources*.

 Getting Ready Test is available online.

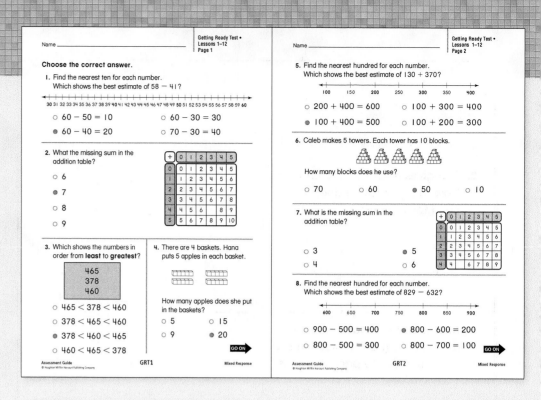

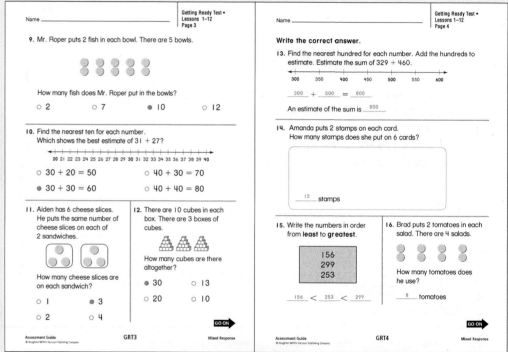

✔ Data-Driven Decision Making ▲ RtI

Item	Lesson	Common Error	Intervene With
1, 23	4	May not understand how to estimate the difference of two 2-digit numbers	R—p. GRR4
2, 7	1	May not understand how to use an addition table	R—p. GRR1
3, 15	6	May not understand how to identify the least or greatest number	R—p. GRR6
4, 24	8	May not understand how to recognize equal groups of 5 and find the total number	R—p. GRR8
5, 13	3	May not understand how to estimate the sum of two 3-digit numbers	R—p. GRR3
6, 12	9	May not understand how to recognize equal groups of 10 and find the total number	R—p. GRR9

Key: R—Getting Ready Lessons and Resources: Reteach

PG74   Planning Guide

Name _____

17. Connor gives 15 stickers to friends. He gives 3 stickers to each friend.

How many friends get stickers?

___5___ friends

18. Find the nearest ten for each number. Add the tens to estimate. Estimate the sum of 34 + 48.

```
30 31 32 33 34 35 36 37 38 39 40 41 42 43 44 45 46 47 48 49 50
```

___30___ + ___50___ = ___80___

An estimate of the sum is ___80___.

19. Sophia uses 10 blocks to build each tower. How many towers can she build with 40 blocks?

___4___ towers

20. Find the nearest hundred for each number. Subtract the hundreds to estimate. Estimate the difference of 825 − 675.

```
600    650    700    750    800    850    900
```

___800___ − ___700___ = ___100___

An estimate of the difference is ___100___.

GO ON

Name _____

21. Mrs. Allen has 12 roses. She puts 3 roses in each vase.

How many vases can she fill?

___4___ vases

22. Avery has 15 pears. She puts the same number of pears in each of 3 baskets.

How many pears are in each basket?

___5___ pears

23. Find the nearest ten for each number. Subtract the tens to estimate. Estimate the difference of 48 − 32.

```
20 21 22 23 24 25 26 27 28 29 30 31 32 33 34 35 36 37 38 39 40 41 42 43 44 45 46 47 48 49 50
```

___50___ − ___30___ = ___20___

An estimate of the difference is ___20___.

24. Hailey puts 5 stars on each bookmark. She makes 6 bookmarks.

How many stars does she use?

___30___ stars

STOP

Portfolio

Portfolio Suggestions The portfolio represents the growth, talents, achievements, and reflections of the mathematics learner. Children might spend a short time selecting work samples for their portfolios.

You may want to have children respond to the following questions:

• Which question was difficult?
• What would you like to learn more about?

For information about how to organize, share, and evaluate portfolios, see the *Chapter Resources*.

✓ Data-Driven Decision Making ⚠ RtI

Item	Lesson	Common Error	Intervene With
8, 20	5	May not understand how to estimate the difference of two 3-digit numbers	R—p. GRR5
9, 16	7	May not understand how to recognize equal groups of 2 and find the total number	R—p. GRR7
10, 18	2	May not understand how to estimate the sum of two 2-digit numbers	R—p. GRR2
11, 22	10	May not understand how to find the number in each group, given the total and the number of groups	R—p. GRR10
14, 19	12	May not understand how to solve word problems involving equal shares	R—p. GRR12
17, 21	11	May not understand how to find the number of groups, given the total and the number in each group	R—p. GRR11

Key: R—Getting Ready Lessons and Resources: Reteach

Hour Before and Hour After

LESSON AT A GLANCE

Lesson Objective
Use clock numbers to find the time 1 hour before and 1 hour after a given time.

Essential Question
How do you tell the time 1 hour before and 1 hour after a given time?

Materials
MathBoard

☑ Animated Math Models
*i*T *i*Tools: Measurement
Ⅷ HMH Mega Math

1 TEACH and TALK 🔘 • Animated Math Models

▶ **Model and Draw** Math Processes and Practices

Materials *i*Tools: Measurement

Use the *i*Tools analog clock or the clocks at the top of the lesson page. Direct children's attention to the clock that shows 8:00.

- **When one hour passes from 7:00 to 8:00, the minute hand moves completely around the clock face once. How far does the hour hand move when this hour passes?** Possible answer: The hour hand moves from one number to the next number on the clock face, or from the 7 to the 8.

Have children indicate the direction in which the clock hands move around the clock face.

- **What would the time be 1 hour after 9:00? Explain.** 10:00; Possible explanation: The hour hand would move from pointing to the 9 to pointing to the 10. **What would the time be 1 hour before 9:00? Explain.** 8:00; Check children's explanations for understanding.

PG76 Planning Guide

This lesson builds on telling time taught in Chapter 7 and prepares children for solving problems involving time intervals taught in Grade 3.

Name _____

Hour Before and Hour After

Essential Question: How do you tell the time 1 hour before and 1 hour after a given time?

Model and Draw

For these times, the minute hand points to the same place. The hour hands point to different numbers.

The time is **8:00**.

The hour hand points to 8.

1 hour before
7:00

The hour hand points to 7.

1 hour after
9:00

The hour hand points to 9.

Share and Show 🔖 MATH BOARD

Write the time shown on the clock. Then write the time 1 hour before and 1 hour after.

Math Talk: The minute hands are the same because they will both be pointing to 12. The hour hands are different because at 8 o'clock it will point to 8 but 1 hour after it will point to 9.

1.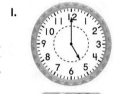

4:00
1 hour before
6:00
1 hour after

5:00

2.

1:30
1 hour before
3:30
1 hour after

2:30

 Math Talk How are the hands on a clock that shows 8 o'clock the same as the hands on a clock 1 hour after? How are they different?

Getting Ready for Grade 3   twenty-nine **GR29**

GR: Practice, p. GRP13

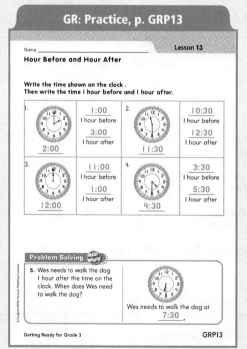

GR: Reteach, p. GRR13

*GR – Getting Ready Lessons and Resources (www.thinkcentral.com)

On Your Own

Write the time shown. Then write the time 1 hour before and 1 hour after.

3.

<u>10:00</u>
1 hour before
<u>12:00</u>
1 hour after

 11:00

4.

<u>9:30</u>
1 hour before
<u>11:30</u>
1 hour after

10:30

5.

<u>12:00</u>
1 hour before
<u>2:00</u>
1 hour after

 1:00

6.

<u>5:30</u>
1 hour before
<u>7:30</u>
1 hour after

6:30

Problem Solving · Real World

7. Tim feeds the cat 1 hour after 7:00. Draw the hour hand and the minute hand to show 1 hour after 7:00. Then write the time.

Tim needs to feed the cat at <u>8:00</u>.

 TAKE HOME ACTIVITY • Ask your child what the time will be 1 hour after 3:30. What time was it 1 hour before 3:30? Have your child tell you how he or she knows.

GR30 thirty

© Houghton Mifflin Harcourt Publishing Company

---

② PRACTICE

▶ **Share and Show** • **Guided Practice**

Before assigning Exercise 2, discuss finding times that are an hour before and an hour after when the initial time is half past an hour. Then ask:

- **When you start at 2:30, and one hour passes, where would the minute hand be pointing?** The minute hand would be pointing at the 6. **Where would the hour hand be pointing?** The hour hand would be pointing halfway between the 3 and the 4. **What time would this be?** 3:30

▶ **On Your Own** • **Independent Practice**

If children answer Exercises 1–2 correctly, assign Exercises 3–6.

- **What is the time 1 hour after 12:00?** 1:00 **How do you know?** Possible answer: I know by the direction that the clock hands move in. The clock hands move toward the 1 after they move past the 12.

▶ **Problem Solving** Real World

UNLOCK THE PROBLEM Have children read the word problem in Exercise 7. After they solve for the time that Tim feeds his cat, make sure children remember to draw clock hands to show this time as well as write this time to complete the sentence.

③ SUMMARIZE

Math Processes and Practices

Essential Question

How can you tell the time 1 hour before and 1 hour after a given time? Possible answer: First you look at where the hour hand is pointing for the given time. Then you think about where the hour hand would point an hour before or an hour after that time.

Math Journal  Math

Draw a clock face that shows 2:00. Write the time. Then write the time that is 1 hour before 2:00 and the time that is 1 hour after 2:00.

LESSON 14

Elapsed Time in Hours

LESSON AT A GLANCE

Lesson Objective
Use a time line to determine elapsed time in hours.

Essential Question
How do you find the number of hours between two times?

Materials
MathBoard

 *iTools: Measurement

---

① TEACH and TALK GO DIGITAL • Animated Math Models

▶ **Model and Draw** Math Processes and Practices

Read the problem. Discuss the time line with children. Point out that this model shows the times from left to right as hours pass and each space between two marks stands for one hour.

• **What times are shown on the clocks?** 2:00, 4:00 **What happens at these times?** practice starts; practice ends

• **On the time line, how many spaces are there from 2:00 P.M. to 4:00 P.M.?** 2 spaces **How many hours passed from 2:00 P.M. to 4:00 P.M.?** 2 hours

② PRACTICE MATH BOARD

▶ **Share and Show • Guided Practice**

Have children read Exercise 1.

• **How many spaces are on the time line from 3:00 P.M. to 6:00 P.M.?** 3 spaces

---

This lesson builds on telling time presented in Chapter 7 and prepares children for solving problems involving time intervals taught in Grade 3.

Name _____

Elapsed Time in Hours

Essential Question How do you find the number of hours between two times?

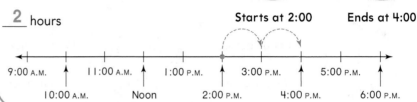

Baseball practice starts at 2:00. Everyone leaves practice at 4:00. How long does baseball practice last?
Use the time line to count how many hours passed from 2:00 P.M. to 4:00 P.M.

__2__ hours

Starts at 2:00   Ends at 4:00

9:00 A.M.   11:00 A.M.   1:00 P.M.   3:00 P.M.   5:00 P.M.
    10:00 A.M.   Noon   2:00 P.M.   4:00 P.M.   6:00 P.M.

 Share and Show MATH BOARD

Use the time line above. Solve.

1. The game starts at 3:00 P.M. It ends at 6:00 P.M. How long does the game last?

__3__ hours

2. The plane leaves at 10:00 A.M. It arrives at 2:00 P.M. How long is the plane trip?

__4__ hours

3. Max goes out at 2:00 P.M. He comes back in at 5:00 P.M. For how long was Max out?

__3__ hours

4. Art class starts at 9:00 A.M. It ends at 11:00 A.M. How long is the art class?

__2__ hours

 Math Talk Describe how you used the time line for Exercise 2.

Possible answer: I started at 10:00 because that's when the plane left. I counted each hour until I ended at 2:00 because that's when it landed.

Getting Ready for Grade 3   thirty-one **GR31**

GR: Practice, p. GRP14

Name _____   Lesson 14

Elapsed Time in Hours

8:00 A.M. 9:00 A.M. 11:00 A.M.   1:00 P.M. 2:00 P.M. 3:00 P.M. 4:00 P.M. 5:00 P.M. 6:00 P.M.
    10:00 A.M.   Noon

Use the time line above. Solve.

1. Eli's grandma comes to visit at 8:00 A.M. She leaves at noon. How long does Eli's grandma visit?

__4__ hours

2. The bus trip starts at 3:00 P.M. and ends at 6:00 P.M. How long is the bus trip?

__3__ hours

3. Mr. North starts mowing the grass at 8:00 A.M. He finishes at 10:00 A.M. How long does Mr. North mow grass?

__2__ hours

4. The movie starts at 2:00 P.M. It ends at 4:00 P.M. How long is the movie?

__2__ hours

Problem Solving Real World

Solve. Draw or write to explain.

5. The times for the events at the science fair are listed.

Event	Time
Set Up Exhibits	1:00 P.M.
Judging	2:30 P.M.
Presentations	4:30 P.M.

Possible answer. I can start to count from when the judging starts and end when presentations begins. 2:30 to 3:30 is 1 hour, then 3:30 to 4:30 makes it 2 hours.

How long will the judging last?   __2__ hours

Getting Ready for Grade 3   GRP14

GR: Reteach, p. GRR14

Name _____   Lesson 14 Reteach

Elapsed Time in Hours

Baseball practice starts at 2:00 P.M. Everyone leaves at 4:00 P.M. How long does baseball practice last?

I can use a time line to count on hours from 2:00 P.M. to 4:00 P.M.

It starts at __2__ :00.   It ends at __4__ :00.

9:00 A.M.   10:00 A.M.   Noon   2:00 3:00 4:00 P.M. 5:00 6:00 P.M.
    11:00 A.M.   1:00 P.M.

So practice lasts __2__ hours.

Use the time line above. Solve.

1. Lisa arrives at the beach at 2:00 P.M. She leaves at 6:00 P.M. How long is Lisa at the beach?

__4__ hours

2. The boat leaves at 3:00 P.M. It gets back at 5:00 P.M. How long is the boat gone?

__2__ hours

3. Kevin starts hiking at 1:00 P.M. He finishes at 3:00 P.M. How long does Kevin hike?

__2__ hours

4. Mrs. Post starts working in the garden at 9:00 A.M. She stops at noon. How long does Mrs. Post work in the garden?

__3__ hours

Reteach   GRR14   Grade 2

---

*GR – Getting Ready Lessons and Resources (*www.thinkcentral.com*)

On Your Own

Use the time line below. Solve.

9:00 A.M.   Noon   3:00 P.M.   6:00 P.M.

5. Paul's baby sister goes to sleep at 4:00 P.M. She wakes up at 6:00 P.M. How long does the baby sleep?

___2___ hours

6. Julia goes to a friend's house at noon. She comes home at 3:00 P.M. How long is Julia gone?

___3___ hours

7. Jeff starts raking leaves at 11:00 A.M. He stops at 1:00 P.M. How long does Jeff rake leaves?

___2___ hours

8. Mom and Carrie arrive at the shopping mall at 1:00 P.M. They leave at 5:00 P.M. How long are they at the mall?

___4___ hours

Problem Solving

Solve. Draw or write to explain.

9. Mr. Norton writes the time for classes on the board.

Class	Time
Math	8:30 A.M.
Reading	9:30 A.M.
Music	11:30 A.M.

How long will reading class last?

Possible answer: I can start to count from when Reading begins and end when Music begins. 9:30 to 10:30 is 1 hour. 10:30 to 11:30 is 1 hour. Reading class will last 2 hours.

___2___ hours

 TAKE HOME ACTIVITY • Ask your child how much time passes between 4:30 and 7:30. Have your child explain how he or she arrived at the answer.

GR32 thirty-two

© Houghton Mifflin Harcourt Publishing Company

▶ **On Your Own** • Independent Practice

If children completed Exercises 1–4 correctly, assign Exercises 5–8. Note that the time line on page GR32 does not have a time label for each mark on the time line. You may wish to have children write times for the unlabeled marks before having them complete these exercises.

After children complete Exercises 5–8, you may wish to challenge them to solve a problem for which they cannot use the time line.

- **Suppose Anthony's family is at a baseball game from 5:00 P.M. to 8:00 P.M. For how many hours are they at the game? Explain how you found your answer.** 3 hours; Check children's explanations for understanding.

▶ **Problem Solving**

UNLOCK THE PROBLEM Read the problem in Exercise 9 together. Explain that for Math class and Reading class, these classes end just when the next class begins. For example, Math class begins at 8:30 A.M. and ends at 9:30 A.M.

3 SUMMARIZE

Math Processes and Practices

Essential Question

How do you find the number of hours between two times? Possible answer: You can use a time line showing hours and count the spaces from one time to the next time.

Math Journal

Draw a time line that shows the hours from 1:00 P.M. to 8:00 P.M. Choose a start time and an end time on your time line for an activity that lasts 4 hours. Describe how you chose the start time and end time.

This lesson builds on telling time presented in Chapter 7 and prepares children for solving problems involving time intervals taught in Grade 3.

LESSON 15

Elapsed Time in Minutes

LESSON AT A GLANCE

Lesson Objective
Use subtraction to find the number of elapsed minutes.

Essential Question
How do you find the number of minutes between two times?

Materials
MathBoard

 iT iTools: Measurement

1 TEACH and TALK GO DIGITAL · Animated Math Models

▶ Model and Draw [Math Processes and Practices]

Discuss the problem in the model with children. Point out that the two times are less than one hour apart, so they are finding the difference between the two times in minutes. Emphasize that this method should only be used when the two times are within the same hour.

- **What times are shown on the two clocks?** 3:15, 3:35 **What happens at these times?** Ken starts cleaning at 3:15 P.M. Ken finishes cleaning at 3:35 P.M.

- **Do you add or subtract to find the number of minutes that pass between 3:15 P.M. and 3:35 P.M.?** subtract

- **Why is 15 subtracted from 35 to solve the problem?** Possible answer: Subtracting 15 minutes from 35 minutes tells how many minutes have passed.

Name _____

Elapsed Time in Minutes

Essential Question How do you find the number of minutes between two times?

Model and Draw

You can use subtraction if the times are within the same hour.

Ken starts cleaning his room at 3:15 P.M. He finishes at 3:35 P.M. How long does it take Ken to clean his room?

$$\begin{array}{r} 35 \\ -15 \\ \hline 20 \end{array}$$

Starts at 3:15 P.M.   Ends at 3:35 P.M.

So it takes Ken __20__ minutes.

Share and Show [MATH BOARD]

Subtract to solve. Show your work.

1. Leah starts eating lunch at 12:10 P.M. She finishes at 12:25 P.M. How long does it take for Leah to eat lunch?

$$\begin{array}{r} 25 \\ -10 \\ \hline 15 \end{array}$$ __15__ minutes

2. Kwan gets on the school bus at 8:10 A.M. He gets to school at 8:55 A.M. How long is Kwan's bus ride?

$$\begin{array}{r} 55 \\ -10 \\ \hline 45 \end{array}$$ __45__ minutes

3. Carla takes her dog to the park at 2:05 P.M. She gets back at 2:40 P.M. How long does Carla walk her dog?

$$\begin{array}{r} 40 \\ -5 \\ \hline 35 \end{array}$$ __35__ minutes

4. Ethan starts his spelling homework at 6:25 P.M. He finishes at 6:45 P.M. How long does Ethan work on his spelling?

$$\begin{array}{r} 45 \\ -25 \\ \hline 20 \end{array}$$ __20__ minutes

 Math Talk How could you check your answers by looking at a clock? Possible answer: I could count by fives to find how many minutes the minute hand moves from one time to the next.

Getting Ready for Grade 3   thirty-three **GR33**

© Houghton Mifflin Harcourt Publishing Company

GR: Practice, p. GRP15

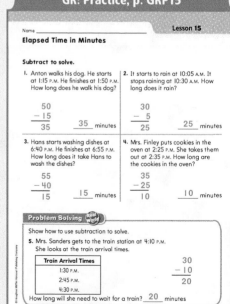

GR: Reteach, p. GRR15

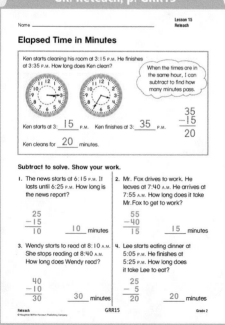

*GR – Getting Ready Lessons and Resources (www.thinkcentral.com)

On Your Own

Subtract to solve. Show your work.

5. Mrs. Hall puts a pizza in the oven at 6:10 P.M. She takes it out at 6:30 P.M. How long does the pizza bake?

$$
\begin{array}{r}
30 \\
-10 \\
\hline
20
\end{array}
$$

__20__ minutes

6. The reading test starts at 1:10 P.M. Everyone must stop at 1:25 P.M. How long do the children have to take their test?

$$
\begin{array}{r}
25 \\
-10 \\
\hline
15
\end{array}
$$

__15__ minutes

7. Kelly starts drawing at 8:15 P.M. She finishes her picture at 8:40 P.M. How long does Kelly draw?

$$
\begin{array}{r}
40 \\
-15 \\
\hline
25
\end{array}
$$

__25__ minutes

8. Tony starts reading at 4:30 P.M. He stops reading at 4:45 P.M. How long does Tony read?

$$
\begin{array}{r}
45 \\
-30 \\
\hline
15
\end{array}
$$

__15__ minutes

Problem Solving

Show how to use **subtraction** to solve.

9. Mr. West gets to the bus stop at 9:05 A.M. He looks at the bus schedule.

Bus Arrival Times
8:30 A.M.
9:30 A.M.
10:30 A.M.

How long will Mr. West need to wait for a bus?

$$
\begin{array}{r}
30 \\
-5 \\
\hline
25
\end{array}
$$

__25__ minutes

 TAKE HOME ACTIVITY • Have your child track how many minutes it would take to do math homework if he or she starts at 5:15 P.M. and stops at 5:45 P.M.

GR34 thirty-four

© Houghton Mifflin Harcourt Publishing Company

---

② PRACTICE

▶ **Share and Show •** Guided Practice

- **Look at Exercise 3. What subtraction will you do to solve the problem?** Possible answer: I will subtract 5 minutes from 40 minutes.

▶ **On Your Own •** Independent Practice

If children completed Exercises 1–4 correctly, assign Exercises 5–8. Remind children that this method should only be used when the two times are within the same hour.

After children complete Exercises 5–8, you may wish to extend the lesson with the following problem:

- **Choose two times between 5:00 P.M. and 5:55 P.M. as the start time and the end time for an activity that lasts 35 minutes. What times did you choose? How did you choose these times?** Check children's explanations for understanding.

▶ **Problem Solving**

UNLOCK THE PROBLEM Have children read the word problem in Exercise 9.

- **When does Mr. West arrive at the bus stop?** 9:05 A.M.
- **After Mr. West gets to the bus stop, at what time will the next bus arrive?** 9:30 A.M. **How do you know?** Possible answer: In the bus arrival schedule, the soonest time after 9:05 A.M. is 9:30 A.M.

③ SUMMARIZE

Math Processes and Practices

Essential Question

How do you find the number of minutes between two times? Possible answer: When both times are within the same hour, you subtract the minutes at the starting time from the minutes at the ending time.

Math Journal   WRITE Math

Write two times between 1:15 P.M. and 1:55 P.M. Subtract to find the number of minutes between the two times. Show your work.

LESSON **16**

Hands On: Capacity • Nonstandard Units

LESSON AT A GLANCE

Lesson Objective
Use a nonstandard unit to measure capacity.

Essential Question
How can you measure how much a container holds?

Materials
MathBoard, small scoops, rice, and various containers (for each small group)

GO DIGITAL

1 TEACH and TALK

▶ **Model and Draw** Math Processes and Practices

Materials: small scoop, rice, various containers

Explain that in this lesson children will be using a scoop as the unit for estimating and measuring how much a container holds. Have children read the directions at the top of the page.

- **Explain in your own words how to use a scoop to measure how much a can holds.**
  Possible answer: You use a scoop to fill the can. You keep track of how many scoops it takes.

- **What are some ways to keep track of the number of scoops?** Possible answers: You can count as you fill the can. You can use tally marks to record the number of scoops.

This lesson builds on measurement skills taught in Chapters 8 and 9 and prepares children for measurement of capacity in standard units taught in Grade 3.

Name _____

Lesson 16

Capacity • Nonstandard Units

Essential Question How can you measure how much a container holds?

Model and Draw

Use a scoop and rice to estimate and measure how much a can holds.

- Estimate how many scoops the can holds.
- Fill a scoop with rice or water.
- Pour it into the can.
- Repeat until the can is full. Keep track of the number of scoops.

Share and Show · MATH BOARD

How many scoops does the container hold? Estimate. Then measure.

Check children's work.

Container	Estimate	Measure
1. mug	about _____ scoops	about _____ scoops
2. vase	about _____ scoops	about _____ scoops
3. paper cup	about _____ scoops	about _____ scoops

Math Talk Explain how you can tell which of the containers on this page is the largest.
Possible answer: I can compare how many scoops of rice they hold. The one that holds the most number of scoops is the largest.

Getting Ready for Grade 3

thirty-five **GR35**

© Houghton Mifflin Harcourt Publishing Company

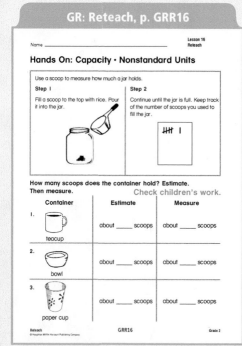

GR: Practice, p. GRP16

Name _____   Lesson 16

Hands On: Capacity • Nonstandard Units

How many scoops does the container hold? Estimate. Then measure. Check children's work.

Container	Estimate	Measure
1. milk carton	about ____ scoops	about ____ scoops
2. measuring cup	about ____ scoops	about ____ scoops
3. sandwich bag	about ____ scoops	about ____ scoops

Problem Solving

Solve.

4. The small box holds 4 scoops of flour. The large box hold 5 more scoops than the small box. How many scoops of flour do the two boxes hold in all?   __13__ scoops in all

Getting Ready for Grade 3   GRP16

GR: Reteach, p. GRR16

Name _____   Lesson 16 Reteach

Hands On: Capacity • Nonstandard Units

Use a scoop to measure how much a jar holds.

Step 1
Fill a scoop to the top with rice. Pour it into the jar.

Step 2
Continue until the jar is full. Keep track of the number of scoops you used to fill the jar.

How many scoops does the container hold? Estimate. Then measure. Check children's work.

Container	Estimate	Measure
1. teacup	about ____ scoops	about ____ scoops
2. bowl	about ____ scoops	about ____ scoops
3. paper cup	about ____ scoops	about ____ scoops

Reteach   GRR16   Grade 2

GR – Getting Ready Lessons and Resources (www.thinkcentral.com)

On Your Own

How many scoops does the container hold? Check children's work.
Estimate. Then measure.

Container	Estimate	Measure
4. jar	about _____ scoops	about _____ scoops
5. milk carton	about _____ scoops	about _____ scoops
6. bowl	about _____ scoops	about _____ scoops

Problem Solving (Real World)

Solve.

7. The red bowl holds 5 scoops of rice. The blue bowl holds twice as much rice as the red bowl. How many scoops of rice do the two bowls hold in all?

15 scoops in all

 TAKE HOME ACTIVITY • Have your child use a paper cup to estimate how much various containers hold. Then check his or her estimate by measuring how much each container holds.

GR36 thirty-six

© Houghton Mifflin Harcourt Publishing Company

2 PRACTICE

▶ Share and Show • Guided Practice

Materials: small scoop, rice, various containers

• **In Exercises 1–3, which container do you estimate will hold the greatest number of scoops of rice? Explain your choice.**
Answers may vary. Check children's answers for reasonableness.

▶ On Your Own • Independent Practice

If children answer Exercises 1–3 correctly, assign Exercises 4–6. You may wish to have a discussion with children about estimation in general. It is important that children understand that there are not *right* and *wrong* estimates; estimation is more about levels of reasonableness.

▶ Problem Solving

UNLOCK THE PROBLEM First have children read the problem in Exercise 7. Then have them write or draw in the workspace to show how they solved the problem.

3 SUMMARIZE

Math Processes and Practices

How can you measure how much a container holds? Possible answer: You can use a scoop as a unit of measure. You keep track of how many units it takes to fill the container.

Math Journal Math

Write a few sentences to describe what you learned about measuring the capacity of a container.

LESSON 17

Describe Measurement Data

LESSON AT A GLANCE

Lesson Objective
Interpret measurement data displayed on a line plot.

Essential Question
What measurement data can a line plot show?

Materials
MathBoard

 GO DIGITAL

☑ Animated Math Models
iT *i*Tools: Graphs
MM HMH Mega Math

1 TEACH and TALK GO DIGITAL • Animated Math Models

▶ Model and Draw Math Processes and Practices

Direct children's attention to the line plot in the model. Review with children the meaning of each of the parts of a line plot: the title, the number labels along the line plot, and the Xs marked on the line plot.

- **What does the line plot show?** Possible answer: The line plot shows the lengths of 12 desks in inches.

- **How can you tell how many desks were measured?** Possible answer: You count all the Xs.

- **How many desks are just 21 inches long?** 1 desk **How do you know?** There is one X above the mark for 21 inches.

PG84   Planning Guide

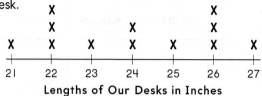

This lesson builds on making line plots of measurement data taught in Chapter 8 and prepares children for using a line plot to display fractional measurements taught in Grade 3.

Name _____

Describe Measurement Data

Essential Question What measurement data can a line plot show?

Model and Draw

A line plot shows data on a number line.

Each X on this line plot stands for the length of 1 desk.

```
                  X                     X
                  X           X         X
      X    X    X    X    X    X    X
    ─┼────┼────┼────┼────┼────┼────┼─
     21   22   23   24   25   26   27
```
Lengths of Our Desks in Inches

_12_ desks were measured.
Two desks are _24_ inches long.

The longest desk is _27_ inches long.
The shortest desk is _21_ inches long.

Share and Show MATH BOARD

Write 3 more sentences to describe Possible answers are given. **what the line plot above shows.**

1. Two more desks are 26 inches long than 27 inches long. _____

2. Five desks are shorter than 24 inches. _____

3. Only one desk is 23 inches long. _____
_____

Write another X above the 23 on the line plot.
Math Talk   Suppose you measured another desk. If the desk was 23 inches long, how could you show this on the line plot above?

Getting Ready for Grade 3   thirty-seven **GR37**

© Houghton Mifflin Harcourt Publishing Company

GR: Practice, p. GRP17

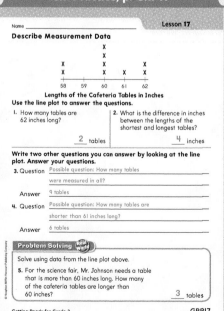

Name _____   Lesson 17
Describe Measurement Data

```
            X
            X                X
      X     X     X    X
    ─┼────┼────┼────┼────┼─
     58   59   60   61   62
```
Lengths of the Cafeteria Tables in Inches
Use the line plot to answer the questions.

1. How many tables are 62 inches long?

2. What is the difference in inches between the lengths of the shortest and longest tables?

    _2_ tables   _4_ inches

Write two other questions you can answer by looking at the line plot. Answer your questions.

3. Question Possible question: How many tables were measured in all?

   Answer 9 tables

4. Question Possible question: How many tables are shorter than 61 inches long?

   Answer 6 tables

Problem Solving

Solve using data from the line plot above.

5. For the science fair, Mr. Johnson needs a table that is more than 60 inches long. How many of the cafeteria tables are longer than 60 inches?   _3_ tables

Getting Ready for Grade 3   GRP17

GR: Reteach, p. GRR17

Name _____   Lesson 17
                                     Reteach
Describe Measurement Data

```
                  X
      X     X     X     X
    ─┼────┼────┼────┼────┼─
     21   22   23   24   25
```
Lengths of Our Desks in Inches

This **line plot** shows the lengths of desks.
Each X stands for the length of 1 desk.

_5_ desks were measured.

_2_ desks are 24 inches long.

```
                  X
            X     X     X
      X     X     X     X
    ─┼────┼────┼────┼────┼─
     4     5     6     7     8
```
Lengths of Our Pencils in Inches

Complete the sentences. Then write two more sentences to describe what the line plot shows.

1. _8_ pencils were measured.

2. _3_ pencils are 7 inches long.

3. Possible answer: One pencil is 4 inches long.
_____

4. Possible answer: The longest pencils are 8 inches long.

Reteach   GRR17   Grade 2
© Houghton Mifflin Harcourt Publishing Company

***GR** – Getting Ready Lessons and Resources (www.thinkcentral.com)*

On Your Own

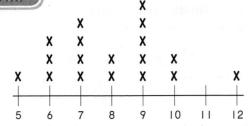

Lengths of Our Classroom Books in Inches

Use the line plot to answer the questions.

4. How many books are 9 and 10 inches in length?

<u> 7 </u> books

5. What is the difference in length between the shortest and longest book?

<u> 7 </u> inches

Write another question you can answer by looking at the line plot. Answer your question.

6. Question <u>Possible question: How many books were measured in all?</u>

Answer <u>   18 books were measured in all.   </u>

Problem Solving Real World

7. Look at the table to the right. It shows Tom's books and their lengths. Add the data for the books to the line plot at the top of the page.

Book	Length
Reading	11 inches
Math	12 inches
Spelling	9 inches

Check line plot above for children's answers.

 TAKE HOME ACTIVITY • Ask your child to explain how to read the line plot on this page.

GR38 thirty-eight

© Houghton Mifflin Harcourt Publishing Company

Getting Ready Lessons and Resources, pp. GR39–GR40   ✓ **Checkpoint**

Name _____

✓ **Checkpoint**

Concepts and Skills

Write the time shown on the clock. Then write the time 1 hour before and 1 hour after.

1.
I hour before <u>2:00</u>
I hour after <u>4:00</u>
3:00

2.
I hour before <u>7:30</u>
I hour after <u>9:30</u>
8:30

2:00 P.M. 3:00 P.M. 4:00 P.M. 5:00 P.M. 6:00 P.M. 7:00 P.M. 8:00 P.M.
Use the time line above. Solve.

3. A movie begins at 2:00 P.M. It is over at 5:00 P.M. How long is the movie?
<u>3</u> hours

4. Madison arrives at a friend's house at 3:00 P.M. She leaves at 7:00 P.M. How long does she stay?
<u>4</u> hours

Getting Ready for Grade 3   thirty-nine **GR39**

Subtract to solve. Show your work.

5. Will arrives at the library at 1:15 P.M. He leaves at 1:50 P.M. How long is Will at the library?
$50 - 15 = 35$ <u>35</u> minutes

6. Andrew begins reading at 3:20 P.M. He stops reading at 3:45 P.M. How long did Andrew read?
$45 - 20 = 25$ <u>25</u> minutes

How many scoops does the container hold? Estimate. Then measure.

7.
Estimate: about ____ scoops
Measure: about ____ scoops
plastic cup
Check children's answers.

8. What is the difference in height between the shortest and tallest plants?
Heights of Plants in Inches
○ 3 inches
◉ 4 inches
○ 5 inches
○ 6 inches

GR40 forty

© Houghton Mifflin Harcourt Publishing Company

---

② PRACTICE

▶ Share and Show • Guided Practice

Before assigning Exercises 1–3, ask children for some examples of sentences that describe the data in the line plot.

▶ On Your Own • Independent Practice

Discuss children's responses in Exercises 1–3 together as a class. Then assign Exercises 4–6. Children use information from the line plot to solve the first two problem. Then they write their own question about the line plot data.

- **What does the line plot on this page show?** The line plot shows the lengths of some classroom books in inches.

- **How did you find the answer to Exercise 5?** Possible answer: I found the difference between the longest book length, 12 inches, and the shortest book length, 5 inches.

▶ Problem Solving Real World

UNLOCK THE PROBLEM Exercise 7 presents a real-life situation involving measurement data. Children then include this additional data in the line plot.

- **After you include this new data in the line plot, how many lengths in all will be shown in the line plot?** 21 lengths

③ SUMMARIZE

Math Processes and Practices

Essential Question

What measurement data can a line plot show? Possible answer: A line plot can show the lengths of objects. It shows how often a given length occurs.

Math Journal   WRITE Math

Draw a line plot for the lengths of several strings in inches. Include Xs for lengths of 5 inches, 6 inches, 7 inches, and 8 inches. Write two sentences to describe the data in your line plot.

Getting Ready for Grade 3 Lesson 17   PG85

LESSON 18

Fraction Models: Thirds and Sixths

LESSON AT A GLANCE

Lesson Objective
Identify thirds and sixths, using fraction models.

Essential Question
How can you identify thirds and sixths?

Materials
MathBoard

iT *i*Tools: Fractions
MM HMH Mega Math

1 TEACH and TALK GO DIGITAL • Animated Math Models

▶ **Model and Draw** Math Processes and Practices

Direct children's attention to the fraction strip showing 3 thirds that are shaded gray. Review how the 3 equal parts make up 1 whole. Then direct children's attention to the fraction strip showing 6 sixths that are shaded gray.

• **When a whole is divided into 6 equal parts, what is each part called?** 1 sixth **How many sixths make up 1 whole?** 6 sixths

2 PRACTICE

▶ **Share and Show** • **Guided Practice**

• **How do you know if a strip is divided into sixths?** Possible answer: If a strip is divided into 6 equal parts, then I know that it is divided into sixths.

This lesson builds on describing equal parts of a whole presented in Chapter 11 and prepares children for work with formal fractions taught in Grade 3.

Name _____

Fraction Models: Thirds and Sixths

Essential Question How can you identify thirds and sixths?

Model and Draw

__3__ equal parts or __3__ thirds

__6__ equal parts or __6__ sixths

__1__ part of 3 equal parts or
__1__ third

__1__ part of 6 equal parts or
__1__ sixth

Share and Show

Answers vary. Check that children color one part in each fraction strip.

Color the strips. Show two different ways to show 1 third.

1.

2.

Color the strips. Show two different ways to show 1 sixth.

3.

4.

Math Talk How are 3 thirds and 6 sixths alike?
Possible answer: Both 3 thirds and 6 sixths make a whole.

Getting Ready for Grade 3   forty-one **GR41**

GR: Practice, p. GRP18

Name _____   Lesson 18
Fraction Models: Thirds and Sixths

Color the strips. Show two different ways to show 5 sixths.
1.   2.

Answers vary. Check that children color five parts in each fraction strip.

Color the strips. Show two different ways to show 2 thirds.
3.   4.

Answers vary. Check that children color two parts in each fraction strip.

Color the strips. Show two different ways to show 3 sixths.
5.   6.

Answers vary. Check that children color three parts in each fraction strip.

Problem Solving Real World

Solve. Write or draw to explain.
7. A sub sandwich is cut into thirds. Jon eats one part of the sandwich. How many parts are left?   __2__ parts

Getting Ready for Grade 3   GRP18

GR: Reteach, p. GRR18

Name _____   Lesson 18
Reteach
Fraction Models: Thirds and Sixths

__3__ equal parts or __3__ thirds

__6__ equal parts or __6__ sixths

There are __3__ equal parts.

There are __6__ equal parts.

__1__ part is shaded.

__1__ part is shaded.

__1__ third is shaded.

__1__ sixth is shaded.

Color the strip. Show one sixth.
1.

Answers vary. Check that children color 1 part in the fraction strip.

Color the strip. Show one third.
2.

Answers vary. Check that children color 1 part in the fraction strip.

Reteach   GRR18   Grade 2

PG86   Planning Guide

*GR – Getting Ready Lessons Thand Resources (www.thinkcentral.com)

On Your Own

Color the strips. Show two different ways to show 2 thirds.

5.

6.

Answers vary. Check that children color two parts in each fraction strip.

Color the strips. Show two different ways to show 2 sixths.

7.

8.

Answers vary. Check that children color two parts in each fraction strip.

Color the strips. Show two different ways to show 3 sixths.

9.

10.

Answers vary. Check that children color three parts in each fraction strip.

Problem Solving Real World

Solve. Write or draw to explain.

11. A sub sandwich is cut into sixths. Tim eats two parts of the sandwich. How many parts are left?

_____4_____ parts left

TAKE HOME ACTIVITY • Have your child draw a picture that shows a slice of cheese divided into thirds.

© Houghton Mifflin Harcourt Publishing Company

GR42 forty-two

▶ **On Your Own** • Independent Practice

If children completed Exercises 1–4 correctly, assign Exercises 5–10.

- **For Exercise 5, how many parts do you need to color to show 2 thirds?** 2 parts
- **Look at Exercises 7 and 8. For each strip, how will you choose which equal parts to color?** Possible answer: For the first strip, I can choose any two of the equal parts to color to show 2 sixths. Then for the next strip, I will color two equal parts that are not in the same positions as the equal parts I shaded on the first strip.

▶ **Problem Solving**

UNLOCK THE PROBLEM Have children read the problem in Exercise 11. Remind children to use the workspace to write or draw to show how they solved the problem.

3 SUMMARIZE

Math Processes and Practices

Essential Question

How can you identify thirds and sixths?
Possible answer: You count the number of equal parts in the whole. Three equal parts are 3 thirds, and each part is one third. Six equal parts are 6 sixths, and each parts is one sixth.

Math Journal  Math

Draw a long rectangle and divide it into thirds. Color to show 2 thirds.

Then draw a long rectangle and divide it into sixths. Color to show 4 sixths.

LESSON 19

Fraction Models: Fourths and Eighths

LESSON AT A GLANCE

Lesson Objective
Identify fourths and eighths, using fraction models.

Essential Question
How can you identify fourths and eighths?

Materials
MathBoard

iT *i*Tools: Fractions

MM HMH Mega Math

1 TEACH and TALK GO DIGITAL • Animated Math Models

▶ Model and Draw Math Processes and Practices

Direct children's attention to the fraction strip showing 4 fourths that are shaded gray. Review how the 4 equal parts make up 1 whole. Then direct children's attention to the fraction strip showing 8 eighths that are shaded gray.

- **When a whole is divided into 8 equal parts, what is each part called?** 1 eighth **How many eighths make up one whole?** 8 eighths

---

This lesson builds on describing equal parts of a whole presented in Chapter 11 and prepares children for work with formal fractions taught in Grade 3.

Name _____

Fraction Models: Fourths and Eighths

Essential Question How can you identify **fourths** and **eighths**?

Model and Draw

__4__ equal parts or __4__ fourths

__8__ equal parts or __8__ eighths

__I__ part of 4 equal parts or __I__ fourth

__I__ part of 8 equal parts or __I__ eighth

Share and Show   MATH BOARD

Answers vary. Check that children color one part in each fraction strip.

Color the strips. Show two different ways to show I fourth.

1.

2.

Color the strips. Show two different ways to show I eighth.

3.

4.

Math Talk How are 4 fourths and 8 eighths alike?
Possible answer: Both 4 fourths and 8 eighths make a whole.

Getting Ready for Grade 3

forty-three **GR43**

GR: Practice, p. GRP19

Name _____   Lesson 19

Fraction Models: Fourths and Eighths

Color the strips. Show two different ways to show 5 eighths.

1.   2.

Answers vary. Check that children color five parts in each fraction strip.

Color the strips. Show two different ways to show 2 fourths.

3.   4.

Answers vary. Check that children color two parts in each fraction strip.

Color the strips. Show two different ways to show 2 eighths.

5.   6.

Answers vary. Check that children color two parts in each fraction strip.

Problem Solving Real World

Solve. Write or draw to explain.

7. A piece of string is cut into fourths. Jenny uses one of the parts to make a bracelet. How many parts of the string are left? ___3___ parts

Getting Ready for Grade 3   GRP19

GR: Reteach, p. GRR19

Name _____   Lesson 19 Reteach

Fraction Models: Fourths and Eighths

__4__ equal parts or __4__ fourths

__8__ equal parts or __8__ eighths

There are __4__ equal parts.

There are __8__ equal parts.

__I__ part is shaded.

__I__ part is shaded.

__I__ fourth is shaded.

__I__ eighth is shaded.

Color the strip. Show one eighth.

1.

Answers vary. Check that children color I part in the fraction strip.

Color the strip. Show one fourth.

2.

Answers vary. Check that children color I part in the fraction strip.

Reteach   GRR19   Grade 2

***GR** – Getting Ready Lessons and Resources (*www.thinkcentral.com*)

On Your Own

Color the strips. Show two different ways to show 2 fourths.

5.

6.

Answers vary. Check that children color two parts in each fraction strip.

Color the strips. Show two different ways to show 3 eighths.

7.

8.

Answers vary. Check that children color three parts in each fraction strip.

Color the strips. Show two different ways to show 5 eighths.

9.

10.

Answers vary. Check that children color five parts in each fraction strip.

Problem Solving

Solve. Write or draw to explain.

11. A loaf of bread is cut into eighths. Jake uses 2 parts to make his lunch. Fran uses 3 parts to make her lunch. How many parts of the loaf are left?

___3___ parts left

TAKE HOME ACTIVITY • Have your child draw a picture to show a slice of cheese divided into fourths.

GR44 forty-four

© Houghton Mifflin Harcourt Publishing Company

2 PRACTICE

▶ Share and Show • Guided Practice

• **How do you know if a strip is divided into eighths?** Possible answer: If a strip is divided into 8 equal parts, then I know that it is divided into eighths.

▶ On Your Own • Independent Practice

If children completed Exercises 1–4 correctly, assign Exercises 5–10.

• **Look at Exercises 9 and 10. For each strip, how many of the equal parts will you not color? Explain your answer.** Possible answer: I will not color 3 of the equal parts on each strip. I will color 5 of the 8 equal parts to show 5 eighths, which leaves 3 of the equal parts without color.

▶ Problem Solving

UNLOCK THE PROBLEM Have children read the problem in Exercise 11. Remind children to use the workspace to write or draw to show how they solved the problem.

3 SUMMARIZE

Math Processes and Practices

Essential Question

How can you identify fourths and eighths?
Possible answer: You count the number of equal parts in the whole. Four equal parts are 4 fourths, and each part is one fourth. Eight equal parts are 8 eighths, and each part is one eighth.

Math Journal

Draw a long rectangle and divide it into fourths. Color to show 3 fourths.

Then draw a long rectangle and divide it into eighths. Color to show 4 eighths.

LESSON 20

Compare Fraction Models

LESSON AT A GLANCE

Lesson Objective
Compare fractions with the use of fraction models.

Essential Question
How can you use fraction models to make comparisons?

Materials
MathBoard

 GO DIGITAL iT *i*Tools: Fractions

---

1 TEACH and TALK **GO DIGITAL** • Animated Math Models

▶ Model and Draw **Math Processes and Practices**

In this lesson, children are introduced to the skill of comparing fractions. It is important to note that the comparisons in this lesson involve pairs of wholes that are the same size. Direct children's attention to the fraction strips in the model. Discuss the shaded part of each strip.

• **How much of the first strip is shaded?** 1 fourth **How much of the second strip is shaded?** 1 half **How do the two shaded parts compare?** The fourth is a smaller part than the half.

• **What do you write to complete the comparison statement below the strips?** Possible answer: You write the symbol for less than. One fourth is less than one half.

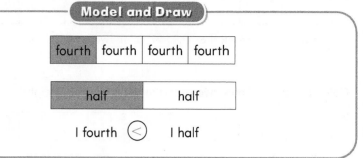

This lesson builds on describing equal parts of a whole presented in Chapter 11 and prepares children for work with comparing fractions taught in Grade 3.

Name _____

Compare Fraction Models

Essential Question How can you use fraction models to make comparisons?

Model and Draw

| fourth | fourth | fourth | fourth |

| half | half |

1 fourth (<) 1 half

Share and Show   MATH BOARD

Color to show the fractions. Write <, =, or >.

1.

1 **half** | half | half |

2 fourths | fourth | fourth | fourth | fourth |

1 half (=) 2 fourths

2.

1 fourth | fourth | fourth | fourth | fourth |

1 eighth | eighth | eighth | eighth | eighth | eighth | eighth | eighth | eighth |

1 fourth (>) 1 eighth

Possible answer: I see that one half is less than three fourths when I compare on the fraction models.

Math Talk Look at the strips above. Is 1 half greater than or less than 3 fourths? How do you know?

Getting Ready for Grade 3   forty-five **GR45**

© Houghton Mifflin Harcourt Publishing Company

GR: Practice, p. GRP20

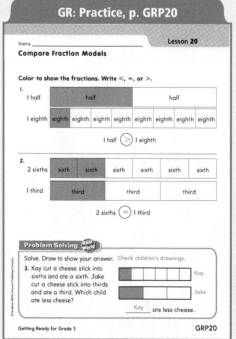

GR: Reteach, p. GRR20

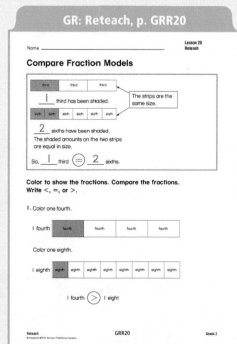

---

*GR – Getting Ready Lessons and Resources (*www.thinkcentral.com*)

On Your Own

Color to show the fractions. Write <, =, or >.

3.

1 third	third	third	third

1 sixth	sixth	sixth	sixth	sixth	sixth	sixth

1 third $>$ 1 sixth

4.

3 sixths	sixth	sixth	sixth	sixth	sixth	sixth

1 half	half	half

3 sixths $=$ 1 half

Problem Solving Real World

Solve. Draw to show your answer.

Check children's drawings.

5. Barry cut a cheese stick into halves and ate a half. Marcy cut a cheese stick into fourths and ate a fourth. Which child ate more cheese?

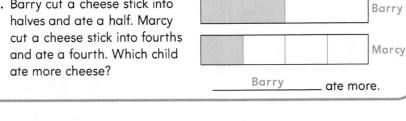

Barry

Marcy

_____Barry_____ ate more.

 TAKE HOME ACTIVITY • Ask your child to draw a picture that shows a square divided into fourths.

GR46 forty-six

© Houghton Mifflin Harcourt Publishing Company

Getting Ready Lessons and Resources, pp. GR47–GR48   ✓ Checkpoint

Name _____

✓ Checkpoint

Concepts and Skills

Color the strips. Show two different ways to show 1 third.

1. | | | | **2.** | | | |

Answers vary. Check that children color 1 part in each fraction strip.

Color the strips. Show two different ways to show 2 sixths.

3. | | | | | | | **4.** | | | | | | |

Answers vary. Check that children color 2 parts in each fraction strip.

Color the strips. Show two different ways to show 2 fourths.

5. | | | | | **6.** | | | | |

Answers vary. Check that children color 2 parts in each fraction strip.

Color the strips. Show two different ways to show 4 eighths.

7. | | | | | | | | | **8.** | | | | | | | | |

Answers vary. Check that children color 4 parts in each fraction strip.

Getting Ready for Grade 3   forty-seven **GR47**

Color to show the fractions. Write >, <, or =.

9. 1 half | half | half |

3 fourths | fourth | fourth | fourth | fourth |

1 half $<$ 3 fourths

10. 1 third | third | third | third |

2 sixths | sixth | sixth | sixth | sixth | sixth | sixth |

1 third $=$ 2 sixths

11. A pizza has 6 slices. Six friends share the pizza equally. What fraction of the pizza does each friend eat?

○ 1 third
○ 2 thirds
● 1 sixth
○ 2 sixths

GR48 forty-eight

---

2 PRACTICE

▶ Share and Show • Guided Practice

Before assigning Exercises 1–2, tell children that when they shade each fraction strip to show each amount, they should begin their shading at the left end of the fraction strip. Refer them to the shaded strips in the model for an example.

- **For Exercise 1, how do you color to show one half?** Possible answer: You find the strip that shows halves and color one of the two equal parts.

▶ On Your Own • Independent Practice

If children complete Exercises 1 and 2 correctly, assign Exercises 3 and 4. Remind children to begin their shading at the left end of the fraction strip so that the shaded parts will be aligned for the visual comparison of each pair of fraction strips.

▶ Problem Solving

UNLOCK THE PROBLEM Have children read the problem in Exercise 5. Tell children that the two shapes (next to the problem) are there to show that the two cheese sticks in the problem are the same size.

- **What comparison statement could you write to show how the amounts compare?** Possible answer: 1 half > 1 fourth

3 SUMMARIZE

Math Processes and Practices

Essential Question

How can you use fraction models to make comparisons? Possible answer: When you have two fraction strips that are the same size, you can shade the strips to show the two amounts. Then you can compare the shaded amounts to know if one amount is greater than the other, or if the amounts are the same.

Math Journal

Look at Exercise 3 on page GR46. Suppose that all of the equal parts on both fraction strips were shaded. Describe how these amounts would compare.

Getting Ready for Grade 3
Test

LESSONS 13 TO 20

Summative Assessment

Use the **Getting Ready Test** to assess children's progress in Getting Ready for Grade 3 Lessons 13–20.

Getting Ready Tests are provided in multiple-choice and mixed-response format in the *Getting Ready Lessons and Resources*.

 Getting Ready Test is available online.

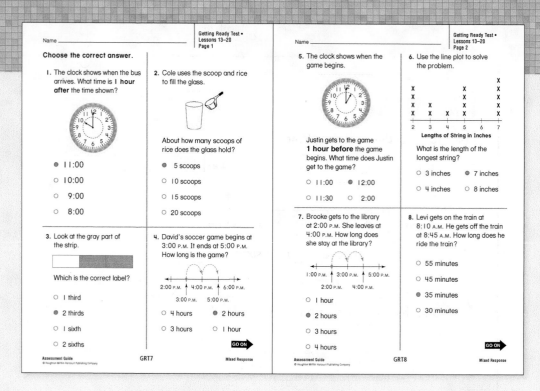

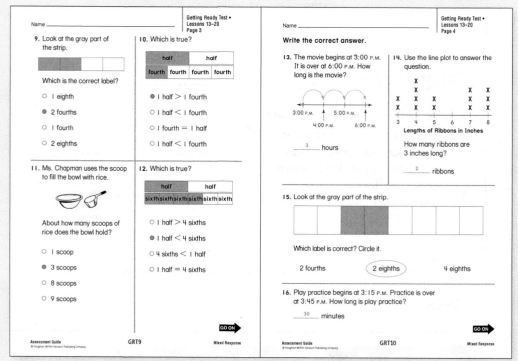

Data-Driven Decision Making

Item	Lesson	Common Error	Intervene With
1, 5, 21	13	May confuse *1 hour before* and *1 hour after* the given time	R—p. GRR13
2, 11, 24	16	May not understand how to make visual connections between nonstandard units of capacity and everyday objects	R—p. GRR16
3, 17, 20	18	May confuse thirds and sixths	R—p. GRR18
4, 7, 13	14	May not understand how to use a time line to find elapsed time in hours	R—p. GRR14

Key: R—Getting Ready Lessons and Resources: Reteach

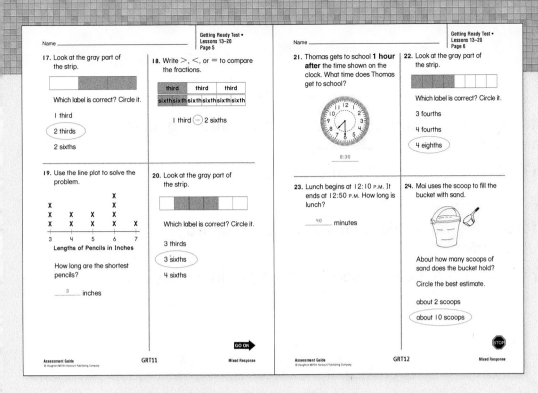

Portfolio Suggestions The portfolio represents the growth, talents, achievements, and reflections of the mathematics learner. Children might spend a short time selecting work samples for their portfolios.

You may want to have children respond to the following questions:

- Which question was difficult?
- What would you like to learn more about?

For information about how to organize, share, and evaluate portfolios, see the *Chapter Resources*.

✓Data-Driven Decision Making ▲RtI

Item	Lesson	Common Error	Intervene With
6, 14, 19	17	May not understand how to use a line plot to solve problems	R—p. GRR17
8, 16, 23	15	May not understand how to subtract to find elapsed time in minutes	R—p. GRR15
9, 15, 22	19	May confuse fourths and eighths	R—p. GRR19
10, 12, 18	20	May confuse comparison symbols	R—p. GRR20

Key: R—Getting Ready Lessons and Resources: Reteach

The Grab-and-Go!™ Differentiated Centers Kit contains ready-to-use readers, games, and math center activities that are designed for flexible usage.

- Readers that integrate math skills with cross-curricular content.

- Games that engage students to practice math skills.

- Math Center Activities that focus on computation, mental math, geometry, measurement, and challenge activities.

See the Grab-and-Go!™ Teacher Guide and Activity Resources for more information.

Chapter		Grade 2	
1 Number Concepts	**Reader**	The Roadside Stand Doubles Fun on the Farm Margo's Lights	
	Game	Four in a Row	
	Activity	Activity 5	Ways to Go Line Time Little Riddles
		Activity 14	We Show Seashells Pattern on Pine Street
		Activity 18	Gone Fishing
2 Numbers to 1,000	**Reader**	Dave and Boots The Number Machine Time to Take a Trip!	
	Game	Fish for Digits! Four in a Row Climb the Steps	
	Activity	Activity 5	Ways to Go Little Riddles
		Activity 18	Out to Dry Seed This! Gone Fishing

Chapter		Grade 2		
3 Basic Facts and Relationships	**Reader**	Doubles Fun on the Farm Benny, Bessie, and the Blueberries Game Time!		
	Game	Caterpillar Chase On the Ferris Wheel		
	Activity	Activity 1		Ring Toss Way to Go! Lucy Goosey
		Activity 3		A Heap of Sheep Quilting Bee Canine Collection
4 2-Digit Addition	**Reader**	Nature's Numbers Butterfly Farm		
	Game	2-Digit Shuffle Soccer Sums		
	Activity	Activity 9		Pebble Beach Marbelous Aqua Addition
		Activity 11		All That Jazz Cool Blades School Store
5 2-Digit Subtraction	**Reader**	Comic Books for Sale Party Plans		
	Game	Subtraction Action What is the Difference?		
	Activity	Activity 5		Ways to Go
		Activity 13		Super Subtraction Measuring Up We're in the Money
		Activity 15		Sticker Subtraction Regrouping

Math Center Activity Cards:

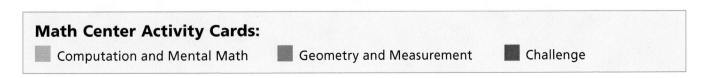 Computation and Mental Math   Geometry and Measurement   Challenge

Chapter		Grade 2	
6 3-Digit Addition and Subtraction	**Reader**	The If Game The Bug Boys	
	Game	Around the World!	
	Activity	Activity 16	Regrouping Ones Hundreds What a Deal
		Activity 19	Zero Gravity Twice is Nice
7 Money and Time	**Reader**	Coin Trick Time to Go Shopping All the Time Is it Time Yet?	
	Game	Tic Tac Total Just in Time!	
	Activity	Activity 6	Piggly Wiggly Mikes Kites Blowing Bubbles
		Activity 8	Time for School Tracking Time
8 Length in Customary Units	**Reader**	Nature Walk	
	Game	How Long?	
	Activity	Activity 17	Super Subs Batter Up!

Chapter	Grade 2		
9 Length in Metric Units	**Reader**	Nature Walk A Trip to the Pond	
	Game	How Long?	
	Activity	Activity 17	Super Subs Batter Up!
10 Data	**Reader**	Wow! Fluffo Sure Can Eat! What Do You Like?	
	Game	Race to Finish	
	Activity	Activity 2	Tally Ho! Keep in Shape Who Knew?
11 Geometry and Fraction Concepts	**Reader**	Building a Mini-Park Square Fair Taking Shape	
	Game	Hidden Figures	
	Activity	Activity 10	Pieced Together In the Right Direction Hexagonal Hopscotch
		Activity 12	Name That Shape! Tina's Recycled Castle Happy Helpers
		Activity 20	Tank Full Toad

Math Center Activity Cards:

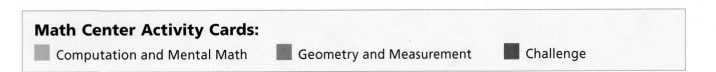

Computation and Mental Math   Geometry and Measurement   Challenge

Sequence Options

Go Math! provides the flexibility to teach the program in a different sequence.
If children need background knowledge for the chapter, use the list of prerequisites.

Chapter	Objectives	Prerequisites
1 Number Concepts	• Classify numbers to 20 as even or odd and write equations with equal addends to represent even numbers. • Write 2-digit numbers in standard form, expanded form, and word form. • Describe 2-digit numbers using place value concepts and find equivalent representations of 2-digit numbers. • Extend counting sequences within 1,000, counting by 1s, 5s, 10s, and 100s.	
2 Numbers to 1,000	• Understand that multiples of 100 are multiples of groups of 10 tens. • Write 3-digit numbers in standard form, expanded form, and word form. • Describe 3-digit numbers using place value concepts and find equivalent representations of 3-digit numbers. • Find 10 more or 10 less than a given 3-digit number; find 100 more or 100 less than a given 3-digit number. • Compare two 3-digit numbers using symbols.	Chapter 1
3 Basic Facts and Relationships	• Apply mental strategies to find sums and differences for basic facts, including the application of the inverse relationship of addition and subtraction. • Apply the Commutative and Associative Properties of Addition to find sums for three 1-digit addends. • Use various representations of addition and subtraction situations, including equations with a symbol for the unknown number. • Write equations to represent the addition of equal groups.	Chapter 1
4 2-Digit Addition	• Apply mental strategies to find sums of two 2-digit numbers. • Use the standard algorithm to find sums of two 2-digit numbers, with and without regrouping. • Use various representations of 2-digit addition situations, including equations with a symbol for the unknown number. • Find sums of three 2-digit numbers; find sums of four 2-digit numbers.	Chapters 1, 3
5 2-Digit Subtraction	• Apply mental strategies to find differences of two 2-digit numbers. • Use the standard algorithm to find differences of two 2-digit numbers, with and without regrouping. • Use various representations of 2-digit subtraction situations, including equations with a symbol for the unknown number.	Chapters 1, 3, 4
6 3-Digit Addition and Subtraction	• Use concrete and pictorial representations to add and subtract 3-digit numbers. • Use the standard algorithm to find sums and differences of 3-digit numbers, with and without regrouping.	Chapters 1–5
7 Money and Time	• Find the total value of a group of coins to $1. • Write money amounts using the ¢ symbol and decimal notation. • Solve word problems involving combinations of dollar bills and coins. • Read and write times shown on analog and digital clocks, including labeling times as a.m. and p.m.	Chapters 1–4

Chapter	Objectives	Prerequisites
8 **Length in Customary Units**	• Measure lengths in inches and in feet, using appropriate tools. • Estimate lengths in inches and in feet. • Solve addition and subtraction problems involving lengths, using number line diagrams and equations with a symbol for the unknown number. • Recognize the inverse relationship between the size and the number of units needed to measure a given length. • Measure the lengths of objects and make a line plot to display the data.	Chapters 1, 3–5
9 **Length in Metric Units**	• Measure lengths in centimeters and meters, using appropriate tools. • Estimate lengths in centimeters and in meters. • Solve addition and subtraction problems involving lengths, using number line diagrams and equations with a symbol for the unknown number. • Recognize the inverse relationship between the size and the number of units needed to measure a given length. • Measure and then find the difference in the lengths of two objects.	Chapters 1, 3–5
10 **Data**	• Collect and record data in tally charts. • Interpret data in picture graphs and bar graphs to solve problems. • Display data in picture graphs and in bar graphs.	Chapters 1, 3
11 **Geometry and Fraction Concepts**	• Identify, describe, and draw three-dimensional shapes, based on attributes of the shapes. • Identify, describe, and draw two-dimensional shapes, based on attributes of the shapes. • Partition rectangles into equal-size squares and find the total number of squares. • Identify, describe, and partition shapes with equal parts that show halves, thirds, or fourths.	

Student Edition Glossary

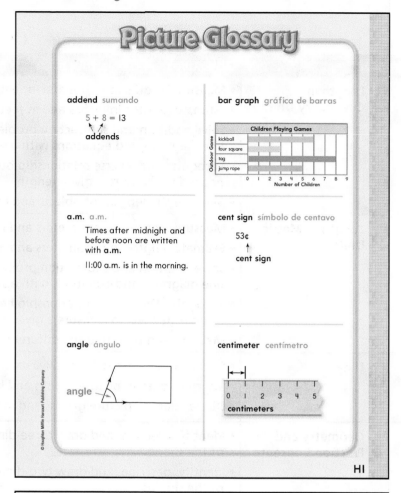

Picture Glossary

addend sumando

$5 + 8 = 13$
↑
addends

a.m. a.m.

Times after midnight and before noon are written with **a.m.**

11:00 a.m. is in the morning.

angle ángulo

angle ⟍

bar graph gráfica de barras

Children Playing Games

Outdoor Game: kickball, four square, tag, jump rope
0 1 2 3 4 5 6 7 8 9
Number of Children

cent sign símbolo de centavo

53¢
↑
cent sign

centimeter centímetro

0 1 2 3 4 5
centimeters

© Houghton Mifflin Harcourt Publishing Company

H1

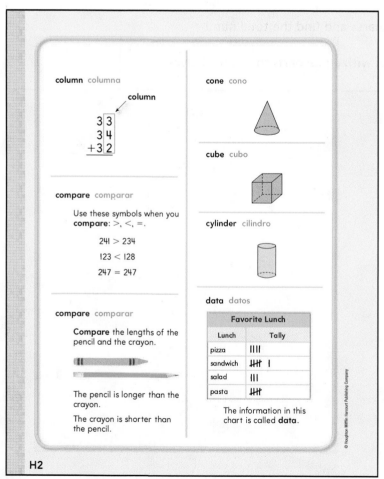

column columna

column
$$\begin{array}{c|c} 3 & 3 \\ 3 & 4 \\ +3 & 2 \end{array}$$

compare comparar

Use these symbols when you **compare**: >, <, =.

241 > 234
123 < 128
247 = 247

compare comparar

Compare the lengths of the pencil and the crayon.

The pencil is longer than the crayon.

The crayon is shorter than the pencil.

cone cono

cube cubo

cylinder cilindro

data datos

Favorite Lunch	
Lunch	Tally
pizza	IIII
sandwich	ⅢⅢ I
salad	III
pasta	ⅢⅢ

The information in this chart is called **data**.

© Houghton Mifflin Harcourt Publishing Company

H2

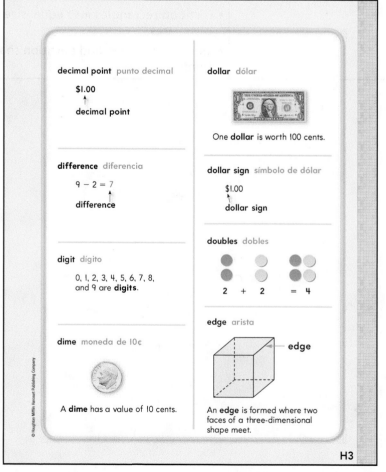

decimal point punto decimal

$1.00
↑
decimal point

difference diferencia

$9 - 2 = 7$
↑
difference

digit dígito

0, 1, 2, 3, 4, 5, 6, 7, 8, and 9 are **digits**.

dime moneda de 10¢

A **dime** has a value of 10 cents.

dollar dólar

One **dollar** is worth 100 cents.

dollar sign símbolo de dólar

$1.00
↑
dollar sign

doubles dobles

2 + 2 = 4

edge arista

edge

An **edge** is formed where two faces of a three-dimensional shape meet.

© Houghton Mifflin Harcourt Publishing Company

H3

PG100 Planning Guide

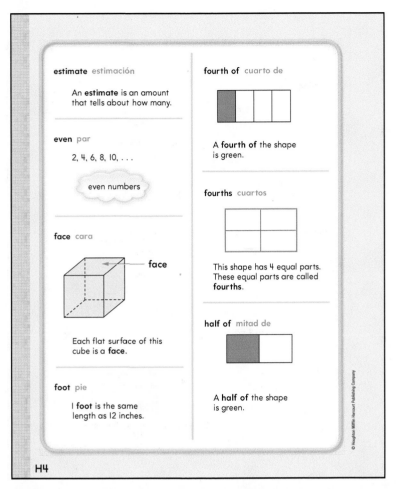

estimate estimación

An **estimate** is an amount that tells about how many.

even par

2, 4, 6, 8, 10, . . .

even numbers

face cara

face

Each flat surface of this cube is a **face**.

foot pie

1 **foot** is the same length as 12 inches.

fourth of cuarto de

A **fourth of** the shape is green.

fourths cuartos

This shape has 4 equal parts. These equal parts are called **fourths.**

half of mitad de

A **half of** the shape is green.

H4

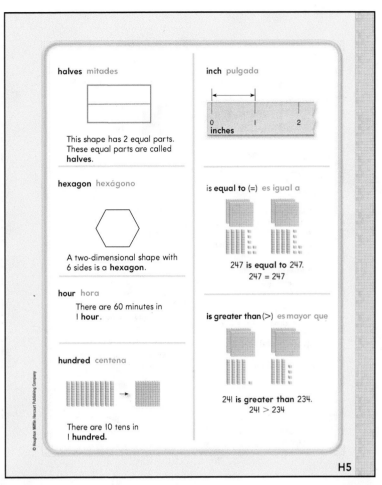

halves mitades

This shape has 2 equal parts. These equal parts are called **halves.**

hexagon hexágono

A two-dimensional shape with 6 sides is a **hexagon.**

hour hora

There are 60 minutes in 1 **hour.**

hundred centena

There are 10 tens in 1 **hundred.**

inch pulgada

inches

is equal to (=) es igual a

247 is equal to 247.
247 = 247

is greater than (>) es mayor que

241 is greater than 234.
241 > 234

H5

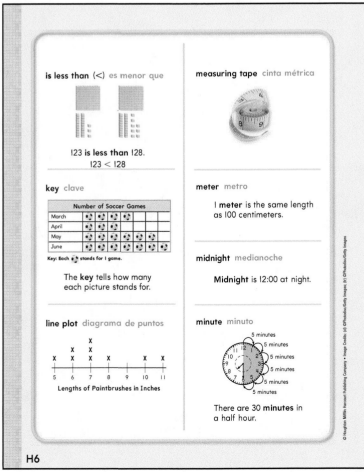

is less than (<) es menor que

123 **is less than** 128.
123 < 128

key clave

Number of Soccer Games					
March					
April					
May					
June					

Key: Each ⚽ stands for 1 game.

The **key** tells how many each picture stands for.

line plot diagrama de puntos

Lengths of Paintbrushes in Inches

measuring tape cinta métrica

meter metro

1 **meter** is the same length as 100 centimeters.

midnight medianoche

Midnight is 12:00 at night.

minute minuto

There are 30 **minutes** in a half hour.

H6

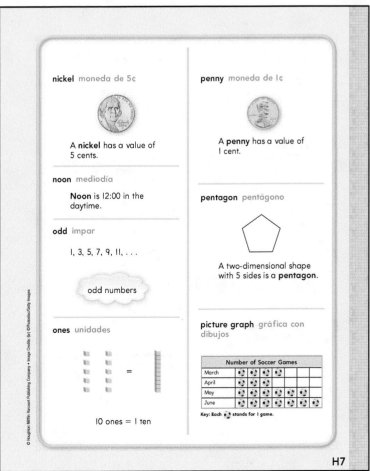

nickel moneda de 5¢

A **nickel** has a value of 5 cents.

noon mediodía

Noon is 12:00 in the daytime.

odd impar

1, 3, 5, 7, 9, 11, . . .

odd numbers

ones unidades

10 ones = 1 ten

penny moneda de 1¢

A **penny** has a value of 1 cent.

pentagon pentágono

A two-dimensional shape with 5 sides is a **pentagon.**

picture graph gráfica con dibujos

Number of Soccer Games					
March					
April					
May					
June					

Key: Each ⚽ stands for 1 game.

H7

Student Edition Glossary continued

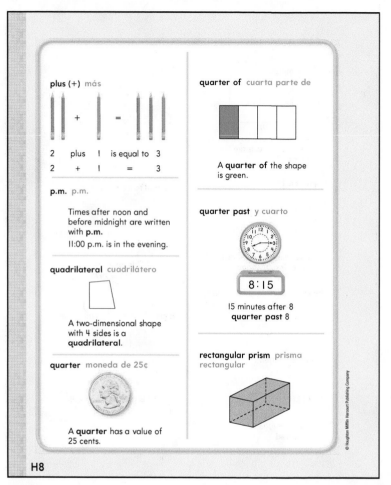

plus (+) más

2   plus   1   is equal to   3
2   +   1   =   3

p.m. p.m.

Times after noon and before midnight are written with **p.m.**
11:00 p.m. is in the evening.

quadrilateral cuadrilátero

A two-dimensional shape with 4 sides is a **quadrilateral**.

quarter moneda de 25¢

A **quarter** has a value of 25 cents.

quarter of cuarta parte de

A **quarter of** the shape is green.

quarter past y cuarto

8:15

15 minutes after 8
quarter past 8

rectangular prism prisma rectangular

© Houghton Mifflin Harcourt Publishing Company

H8

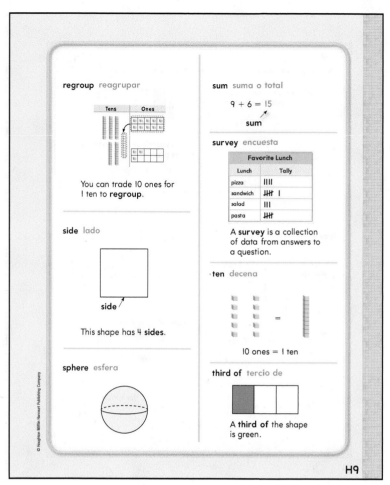

regroup reagrupar

Tens	Ones

You can trade 10 ones for 1 ten to **regroup**.

side lado

side

This shape has 4 **sides**.

sphere esfera

sum suma o total

$9 + 6 = 15$

sum

survey encuesta

Favorite Lunch	
Lunch	Tally
pizza	IIII
sandwich	ЖН I
salad	III
pasta	ЖН

A **survey** is a collection of data from answers to a question.

ten decena

=

10 ones = 1 ten

third of tercio de

A **third of** the shape is green.

© Houghton Mifflin Harcourt Publishing Company

H9

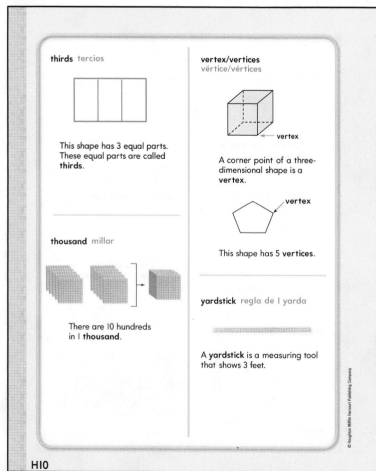

thirds tercios

This shape has 3 equal parts. These equal parts are called **thirds**.

thousand millar

There are 10 hundreds in 1 **thousand**.

vertex/vertices vértice/vértices

vertex

A corner point of a three-dimensional shape is a **vertex**.

vertex

This shape has 5 **vertices**.

yardstick regla de 1 yarda

A **yardstick** is a measuring tool that shows 3 feet.

© Houghton Mifflin Harcourt Publishing Company

H10

Teacher Notes

Professional Development References

Baldi, S., Jin, Y., Skemer, M., Green, P. J., & Herget, D. (2007). *Highlights from PISA 2006: Performance of U.S. 15-year-old students in science and mathematics literacy in an international context* (NCES-2008-016). National Center for Education Statistics, Institute of Education Sciences. Washington, DC: U.S. Department of Education.

Battista, M. (2007). The development of geometric and spatial thinking. In F. K. Lester (Ed.), *Second handbook of research on mathematics teaching and learning: Volume 2* (pp. 843–908). Charlotte, NC: Information Age Publishing.

Cathcart, W. G., Pothier, Y. M., Vance, J. H., & Bezuk, N. S. (2006). *Learning mathematics in elementary and middle schools.* Columbus, OH: Pearson.

Clements, D. H., & Sarama, J. (2014). *Learning and teaching early math: The learning trajectories approach.* New York: Routledge, Taylor and Francis.

Furhman, S. H., Resnick, L., & Shepard, L. (2009). Standards aren't enough. *Education Week, 29*(7), 28.

Fuson, K.C. (2003). Developing mathematical power in whole number operations. In J. Kilpatrick, W. G. Martin, & D. Schifter (Eds.), *A research companion to principles and standards for school mathematics* (pp. 68–94). Reston, VA: NCTM

Geist, E. (2009). *Children are born mathematicians: Supporting mathematical development, birth to age 8.* Columbus, OH: Pearson.

Gonzales, P., Williams, T., Jocelyn, L., Roey, S., Katsberg, D., & Brenwald, S. (2008). *Highlights from TIMSS 2007: Mathematics and science achievement of U.S. fourth- and eighth-grade students in an international context* (NCES 2009-001 Revised). National Center for Education Statistics, Institute of Education Sciences. Washington, DC: U.S. Department of Education.

Martinez, J. G. R., & Martinez, N.C. (2007). *Teaching mathematics in elementary and middle school.* Upper Saddle River, NJ: Pearson Merrill Prentice Hall.

Marzano, R. J. (2003). *What works in schools: Translating research into action.* Alexandria, VA: ASCD.

National Council of Teachers of Mathematics. (2000). *Principles and standards for school mathematics.* Reston, VA: Author.

National Council of Teachers of Mathematics (2014). *Principles to Actions: Ensuring Mathematical Success for All.* Reston, VA: Author.

National Council of Teachers of Mathematics. (2005). *Standards and Curriculum: A view from the nation, a joint report by the National Council of Teachers of Mathematics (NCTM) and the Association of State Supervisors of Mathematics (ASSM).* J. W. Lott & K. Nishimura (Eds.). Reston, VA: Author.

National Mathematics Advisory Panel. (2008). *Foundations for success: The final report of the National Mathematics Advisory Panel.* Washington, DC: U. S. Department of Education.

National Research Council. (2001). *Adding it up: Helping children learn mathematics.* J. Kilpatrick, J. Swafford, & B. Findell (Eds.). Washington, DC: National Academy Press.

Reed, D. S. (2009). Is there an expectations gap? Educational federalism and the demographic distribution of proficiency cut scores. *American Educational Research Journal, 46*(3), 718–742.

Resnick, Lauren B. (1983). A developmental theory of number understanding. In H. P. Ginsberg (Ed.), *The development of mathematical thinking* (pp. 109-151). New York: Academic Press.

Reys, B. J., Chval, K., Dingman, S., McNaught, M., Regis, T. P., & Togashi, J. (2007). Grade-level learning expectations: A new challenge for elementary mathematics teachers. *Teaching Children Mathematics, 14*(1), 6–11.

Schmoker, M. (2011). Focus: Elevating the essentials to radically improve student learning. Alexandria, VA: ASCD.

Schneider, M. (2007). *National Assessment of Education Progress: Mapping 2005 state proficiency standards onto the NAEP scales.* Washington, DC: IES National Center for Education Statistics.

Troutman, A. P., & Lichtenberg, B.K. (2003). *Mathematics: A good beginning* (6th ed.). Belmont, CA: Thomson

Van de Walle, J. A. (2004). *Elementary and middle school mathematics: Teaching developmentally* (5th ed.). Boston, MA: Pearson Education.

Van de Walle, J. A. (2006). *Elementary and middle school mathematics: Teaching developmentally* (6th ed.). Boston, MA: Pearson.

Van de Walle, J. A., & Lovin, L. H. (2007). *Teaching student-centered mathematics: Grades K-3.* Boston: Allyn & Bacon Professional.

Teacher Notes

Index

Chapter Book 1	pages 1A–70B
Chapter Book 2	pages 71A–150B
Chapter Book 3	pages 151A–232B
Chapter Book 4	pages 233A–312B
Chapter Book 5	pages 313A–386B
Chapter Book 6	pages 387A–454B
Chapter Book 7	pages 455A–536B
Chapter Book 8	pages 537A–598B
Chapter Book 9	pages 599A–648B
Chapter Book 10	pages 649A–692B
Chapter Book 11	pages 693A–750B
Planning Guide	pages PG4–PG124

About Go Math!, Program Overview, *PG4–PG40*

About the Math

If Children Ask, 37A, 193A, 243A, 273A, 285A, 353A, 377A, 421A, 445A, 527A, 553A, 615A, 697A, 747A

Teaching for Depth, 13A, 19A, 55A, 75A, 117A, 123A, 159E, 223A, 249A, 267A, 297A, 317A, 323A, 329A, 347A, 391A, 397A, 409A, 415A, 427A, 439A, 463A, 463E, 467A, 491A, 497A, 503A, 515A, 559A, 571A, 589A, 599E, 627A, 633A, 671A, 677A, 753A, 759A

Why Teach This, 25A, 31A, 49A, 87A, 99A, 163A, 169A, 181A, 237A, 255A, 279A, 291A, 341A, 365A, 371A, 479A, 521A, 547A, 565A, 577A, 609A, 639A, 653A, 659A, 697A, 729A, 741A

Access Prior Knowledge, *In every Teacher Edition lesson. Some examples are: 25B, 87B, 163B, 237B, 341B, 521B, 659B*

Act It Out strategy, 217–220, 503–506

Activities

ELL Vocabulary Activity. See Developing Math Language

Games. *See* Games

Grab and Go!™ Differentiated Centers Kit, In every Teacher Guide lesson. Some examples are: 39, 78, 172, 288, 400, 412, 518, 612, 708

Hands On Activities, 13, 19, 31, 43, 87, 237, 255, 329, 335, 403, 409, 427, 467, 473, 479, 485, 541, 547, 553, 571, 583, 589, 603, 609, 615, 627, 639, 653, 665, 671, 723, 729, 735, 741, 747

Independent Activities, 16, 22, 28, 34, 39, 46, 52, 58, 64, 74, 78, 84, 90, 96, 102, 108, 120, 126, 132, 138, 144, 166, 172, 178, 184, 190, 195, 202, 208, 214, 220, 226, 240, 246, 252, 258, 264, 270, 275, 282, 288, 294, 300, 306, 320, 326, 332, 338, 344, 349, 356, 362, 368, 374, 380, 388, 394, 400, 406, 412, 417, 424, 430, 436, 442, 448, 470, 476, 482, 493, 500, 506, 512, 518, 524, 530, 544, 550, 556, 562, 580, 586, 606, 612, 618, 623, 630, 636, 642, 656, 662, 667, 674, 680, 686, 708, 714, 720, 726, 738, 743, 750, 768

Take Home Activity, 16, 22, 28, 34, 39, 46, 52, 58, 64, 78, 84, 90, 96, 102, 108, 113, 120, 126, 132, 138, 144, 166, 172, 178, 184, 190, 195, 202, 208, 214, 220, 226, 240, 246, 252, 258, 270, 275, 282, 288, 294, 300, 306, 320, 326, 332, 338, 344, 349, 356, 362, 368, 374, 380, 394, 400, 406, 412, 417, 424, 430, 436, 442, 448, 470, 476, 482, 488, 493, 500, 506, 512, 518, 524, 530, 544, 550, 556, 562, 574, 580, 586, 592, 606, 612, 618, 630, 636, 642, 656, 662, 667, 674, 680, 686, 708, 714, 720, 726, 732, 738, 743, 750, 756, 762, 768

Addends

adding 3 one-digit, 181–184, *297A*

adding 3 two-digit, 297–300

adding 4 two-digit, 303–306

breaking apart to add, 176–177, 237–240, 249–252, 397–400

defined, *159H*, 170, *387H*

identifying, 169A, 193A, 267A

missing, See Addends, unknown

order of, 169–172, 181–184, 297–300, 303–306

unknown, 183, 194, 212–214, 232, 285–287, 292–293, 300, 305, 309, 371–373, 622–623, 648

Addition

adding three 1-digit addends, 181–184

addition words, 255A

alternative algorithms for, 313E

Associative Property, 181A

basic facts, 163–166, *169A*, 169–172, 175–178, 181–184, 187–190, *199B, 211B*, 211–214, *229–230, 243B, 273B, 347B, 503B, 577B, 583B, 615B*

Commutative Property, 169A, 169, 181A, 217A

concepts, 9E, 159E

doubles and near doubles facts, 163–166

of equal groups, 217–220, *223A*, 223–226, 366–368

to find differences, 187–189, 359–362

finding sums of 3 two-digit numbers, 297–300

finding sums of 4 two-digit numbers, 303–306

of length, 565–567, *621A*, 621–623

lining up the digits in, 279A, 279

make a ten, 175–178, 182–184

missing addends, 177, 183, 194–195, 208, 212, 213, 232, 246, 252, 257, 264, 282, 285, *285*, 286, 287, 292, 293, *293*, 311, 312, 332, 347, 367, 374, 380, 385, 386, 422, 430, 433, 442, 448, 453, 606, 661, 756

model

bar model, *187A*, 187–188, 205–207, *285A*, 285–288, 377–380

make a ten to add, 177

regrouping, 255–258

Most Difficult 2-Digit Addition Problem, 274

part-whole relationships, 31A

place value, 9E, 93A, 99A, 135A, 169A, 397A

regrouping in, 255–258, 261–264, 267–270, 273–275, 280–282, 297–300, 303–306, *337,* 403–406, 409–412, 415–417

repeated, *697A*

standard algorithm for, *261A, 267A, 279A, 427A*

strategies

breaking apart addends to add, 176–177, 237–240, 249–252, 397–400

compensation, 243A

doubles and near doubles, *159E, 163A,* 163–166

invented, 313E

make a ten, *159E,* 175–178, 182–184, *233E*

use related facts, 187–190

using diagrams, 285A

subtraction related to, *159E,* 187–190, *193A, 313E,* 359–362

three-digit numbers

breaking apart to add, 397–400, *485A*

drawing to represent, 391–394

regrouping, 403–406, 409–412, 415–417

of three or more addends, 181–184, *297A,* 297–300, *303A,* 303–306

two-digit numbers

breaking apart addends to add, 237–240, 249–252

diagrams for, *285A,* 285–288

in equations, *291A,* 291–294

modeling and recording, 261–264

regrouping, 255–261, 273–275

strategies for, 243–246, 267–270, *285A*

three or more addends, *297A,* 297–300, 303–306

vertical addition, 279–282

using models and quick pictures, 237–238, 243, 255–258, 261–264, 267, 329, 335–338, 341, 391–394, 397, 403, 409, 419, 421, 427, 433

write equations to represent problems, 205–208, 211–214, 285–288, 291–294

writing vertically, *279A,* 279–282

Addition facts

doubles facts, *159E, 163A*

doubles minus one facts, *159E, 163A*

doubles plus one facts, *159E, 163A*

to find subtraction fact, *193A*

Advanced Learners, *In most Teacher Edition lessons. Some examples are: 14, 164, 318, 468, 604, 654, 706*

Algebraic thinking

adding four addends, *303A,* 303–306

adding three addends, *181A,* 181–184, *297A,* 297–300

breaking apart numbers to subtract, *317A,* 317–320, *323A,* 323–326

comparing numbers, *141A,* 141–144

different names for numbers, *43A,* 43–46, *49A,* 49–52

different ways to show numbers, *117A,* 117–120

even and odd numbers, *13A,* 13–16, *19A,* 19–22

making a ten to add, *175A,* 175–178

number patterns, *129A,* 129–132

relating addition to subtraction, *187A,* 187–190

repeated addition, *223A,* 223–226

using drawings to represent problems, *205A,* 205–208

using equations to represent problems, *211A,* 211–214

writing equations to represent addition, *291A,* 291–294

writing equations to represent subtraction, *371A,* 371–374

Algorithms

alternative, 237–240, 243–246, 249–252, 317–320, 323–326, 397–400

standard, 261–264, 267–270, 273–275, 279–282, 335–338, 341–344, 347–349, 353–356, 403–406, 409–412, 415–417, 421–424, 427–430, 433–436

a.m., *463H, 527A,* 527–530

Analog clocks, 509–512, 515–518, 521–524, 527–530

Analyze, 319, 326, 338, 448, 470, 719

Analyze Relationships, *144,* 240, 282, *326, 338,* 556, 642

Angles

defined, *701H,* 730

in two-dimensional shapes, *729A,* 729–732, 735–738

Animated Math Models, *In most Teacher Edition lessons. Some examples are: 13, 99, 255, 415, 615, 693, 705*

Apply, *102,* 586, 655

Area, *of rectangles, 741A*

Assessment

Assessing Prior Knowledge, 10, 72, 160, 234, 314, 388, 464, 538, 600, 650, 702

Chapter At A Glance, 9C, 71C, 159C, 233C, 313C, 387C, 463C, 537C, 599C, 649C, 701C

Chapter Review/Test, 67–70, 147–150, 229–232, 309–312, 383–386, 451–454, 533–536, 595–598, 645–648, 689–692, 771–774

Teacher Edition and Planning Guide references in *italics*; Planning Guide references begin with PG

Diagnostic Assessment
> Diagnostic Interview Task, *10, 72, 160, 234, 314, 388, 464, 538, 600, 650, 702*
>
> Quick Check, *In every Teacher Guide lesson. Some examples are: 32, 88, 250, 410, 528, 666, 742*
>
> Show What You Know, 10, 72, 160, 234, 314, 388, 464, 538, 600, 650, 702

Formative Assessment
> Mid-Chapter Checkpoint, 40, 114, 196, 276, 350, 418, 494, 568, 624, 668, 744
>
> Personal Math Trainer, *In every Teacher Guide lesson. Some examples are: 10, 100, 276, 350, 494, 568, 600, 668*

Summative Assessment
> Chapter Review/Test, 67–70, 147–150, 229–232, 309–312, 383–386, 451–454, 533–536, 595–598, 645–648, 689–692, 771–774
>
> Chapter Test, *70A–70B, 150A–150B, 232A–232B, 312A–312B, 386A–386B, 454A–454B, 536A–536B, 598A–598B, 648A–648B, 692A–692B, 774A–774B*

Assessment, Diagnosis, Intervention, *PG14*

Associative Property, *181A*

Authors, Consultants, and Advisory Board, *PG16–PG17*

Bar graphs
> defined, *649H*, 672
> making, *677A*, 677–680, *683A*, 683–686
> picture graphs compared with, *671A*
> reading, 671–674
> using to solve problems, 671–674, 677–680, 683–686

Bar models
> addition problems, 187–188, *205A*, 205–208, *285A*, 285–288, 291, 377–380
> multistep problems, 377–380
> subtraction problems, 205–208, *365A*, 365–368, 377–380

Basic Facts. *See Problem of the Day*

Basic Facts, 163–166, 169–172, 175–178, 181–184, 187–190, 193–195, 199–202, 205–208, 211–214

Big Idea
> At a Glance, Big Idea, 1A–1B, 151A–151B, 455A–455B, 693A–693B
> Connections, 8A, 158A, 462A, 700A
> Digital Path, 1C–1D, 151C–151D, 455C–455D, 693C–693D
> Projects, 158B, 462B, 700B

Review Projects, *PG44–PG49*

Vocabulary Story, *1–8, 151–158, 455–462, 693–700*

Big Idea At a Glance, *1A–1B, 151A–151B, 455A–455B, 693A–693B*

Break Apart strategy addition, 176–177, 237–240, 249–252, 397–400
> subtraction, 317–320, 323–326

Calendar Math. *See Problem of the Day*

Centimeters, *599H*, 603–606, 609–612, 615–618, 621–624, *627A*, 627–630

Cent sign, *463H*, 468–470, 473–476, 479–482, 485–488, 491, 497

Chapter Essential Questions. *See Essential Question, Chapter*

Chapter, Introduce the, *9, 71, 159, 233, 313, 387, 463, 537, 599, 649, 701*

Chapter at a Glance, *9A–9D, 71A–71C, 159A–159D, 233A–233D, 313A–313D, 387A–387D, 463A–463D, 537A–537D, 599A–599D, 649A–649C, 701A–701D*

Chapter Review/Test, 67–70, 147–150, 229–232, 309–312, 383–386, 451–454, 533–536, 595–598, 645–648, 689–692, 771–774

Chapter Test, *70A–70B, 150A–150B, 232A–232B, 312A–312B, 386A–386B, 454A–454B, 536A–536B, 598A–598B, 648A–648B, 692A–692B, 774A–774B*

Chapter Vocabulary, *9H, 71H, 159H, 233H, 313H, 387H, 463H, 537H, 599H, 649H, 701H*

Circles, 705, 711

Classroom Management, Daily, *9F, 71F, 159F, 313F, 387F, 463F, 537F, 599F, 649F, 701F*

Clocks, *509A*, 509–512, 515–518, 521–524, 527–530, *761*

Coherence, *In every Teacher Edition Lesson. Some examples are: 61A, 141A, 181A, 237A, 323A, 467, 571A, 701A*

Coins
> cent sign, 468–470, 473–476, 479–482, 485–488, 491, 497
> counting, *463A, 467A*, 467–470, *473A, 479A*, 479–482, *485A*, 485–488, *491A, 499*
> dimes, 467–470, 473–476, 479–482, 485–488, 491–493, 497–500, 503–506
> nickels, 467–470, 473–476, 479–482, 485–488, 491–493, 497–500, 503–506
> pennies, 467–470, 473–476, 479–482, 485–488, 491–493, 497–500, 503–506
> quarters, 473–476, 479–482, 485–488, 492–493, 497–500

Common Errors, *14, 20, 26, 32, 38, 44, 50, 56, 62, 76, 82, 88, 94, 100, 106, 112, 118, 124, 130, 136, 142, 164, 170, 176, 182, 188, 194, 200, 206, 212, 218, 224, 238, 244, 250, 256, 262, 268, 274, 280, 286, 292, 298, 304, 318, 324, 330, 336, 342, 348, 354, 360, 366, 372, 378, 392, 398, 404, 410, 416, 422, 428, 434, 440, 446, 468, 474, 480, 486, 492, 498, 504, 510, 516, 522, 528, 542, 548, 554, 560, 566, 572, 578, 584, 590, 604, 610, 616, 622, 628, 634, 640, 654, 660, 666, 672, 678, 684, 706, 712, 718, 724, 730, 736, 742, 748, 754, 760, 766*

Communicate math ideas. *See* Math Talk; Writing

Commutative Property of Addition, *169A,* 169–172, *181A*

Compare
defined, *71H,* 142
numbers, *135A,* 135–138, 141–144
numbers using symbols, 142–144

Compensation, *243A*

Cones, *701H,* 705–708, 711, 717, 774

Congruence, *697A*

Correlations
to Go Math! Sequence Options, PG98–PG99
to Grab-and-Go™ Differentiated Centers Kit, PG94–PG97

Counting
coins to find total value, 467–470, 473–476, 479–482, 485–488, 493, 497–499
count back, 81A, 159I
count on, 9E, 81A, 159E, 159I
count on and count back by 10, 123–126
count on and count back by 100, 123–126
money, 463E, 467A, 473A, 479A, 485A, 491A
orally, 129A
by 1s, 55–58, 61, 468
by 5s, 55–58, 61–64, 468, *649I, 665A*
by 10s, 55–58, 61–64, 129–132, 468, *649I, 665A*
by 100s, 61–64, 129–132

Counting patterns
within 100, 55–58
within 1,000, 61–64, 128–132

Cross-Curricular Connections and Activities
Connections to Science, 8A, 158A, 462A

Cubes
building rectangular prisms from, 718–720
faces, edges, and vertices, 711–714
identify and describe, *701H,* 705–708, 717

Curious About Math, 9, 71, 159, 233, 313, 387, 463, 537, 599, 649, 701

Curved surfaces, 717

Cylinders, *701H,* 705–708, 711, 717

Daily Classroom Management, *9F, 71F, 159F, 233F, 313F, 387F, 463F, 537F, 599F, 649F, 701F*

Daily Routines
Fluency Builder, In most Teacher Edition lessons. Some examples are: 25B, 55B, 223B, 409B, 445B, 547B, 765B
Problem of the Day
Basic Facts, 205B, 211B, 273B, 291B, 329B, 347B, 365B, 377B, 391B, 415B, 427B, 503B, 553B, 559B, 565B, 577B, 615B, 627B, 659B, 753B
Calendar Math, 13B, 25B, 37B, 55B, 81B, 93B, 111B, 193B, 237B, 285B, 297B, 303B, 323B, 335B, 353B, 433B, 445B, 467B, 485B, 603B, 697B
Number of the Day, 19B, 31B, 43B, 49B, 61B, 75B, 87B, 117B, 123B, 163B, 169B, 181B, 187B, 217B, 243B, 249B, 255B, 261B, 279B, 317B, 341B, 359B, 371B, 397B, 409B, 421B, 439B, 463B, 491B, 497B, 509B, 521B, 541B, 571B, 589B, 609B, 621B, 653B, 665B, 671B, 683B, 697B, 705B, 729B, 735B, 759B, 765B
Secret Code Cards, 99B
Word of the Day, 105B, 129B, 135B, 223B, 267B, 403B, 479B, 515B, 527B, 547B, 583B, 633B, 639B, 677B, 741B, 747B
Vocabulary Builder, 75B, 99B, 105B, 141B, 163B, 169B, 255B, 267B, 273B, 297B, 317B, 341B, 347B, 391B, 415B, 467B, 491B, 571B, 577B, 627B, 639B, 653B, 671B, 729B, 747B

Data
bar graphs
defined, *649H,* 672
interpreting, *671A,* 671–674
making, *677A,* 677–680, *683A,* 683–686
picture graphs compared with, *671A*
using to solve problems, 671–674, 677–680, 683–686
defined, 649H
line plots, 589–592
picture graphs
defined, 660
making, 665–667
reading, 659–662
using to solve problems, 659–662, 665–667, 671
surveys, 653–656, *677A*
tally charts, *653A,* 653–656, 659, 666–667

Data Analysis
bar graphs, *671A*, 671–674, *677A*, 677–680, *683A*, 683–686
decision making based on, 649E
graph scales, 677A
pictorial representation, 589A
value and frequency, 649E

Data-Driven Decision Making, 40, 67–68, 70A–70B, 114,
147–148, 150A–150B, 196, 229–230, 232A–232B, 276,
309–310, 312A–312B, 350, 383–384, 386A–386B, 418,
451–454, 454A–454B, 494, 533–534, 536A–536B, 568,
595–596, 598A–598B, 624, 645–646, 648A–648B, 668,
689–690, 692A–692B, 744, 771–774, 774A–774B

Decimal notation, for money, *463E, 463H, 492–493, 497A,*
498–500, *499,* **503–506**

Decimal system, *metric units and, 615A*

Developing Math Language, *9H, 71H, 159H, 233H, 313H,*
387H, 463H, 537H, 599H, 649H, 701H

Diagnostic Assessment, 10, 72, 160, 234, 314, 388, 464, 538,
600, 650, 702

Diagnostic Interview Task, 10, 72, 160, 234, 314, 388, 464,
538, 600, 650, 702

Difference, *159H, 313H*

Differentiated Instruction
Advanced Learners, In most Teacher Edition lessons. Some
examples are: 14, 164, 318, 468, 604, 654, 706
Daily Classroom Management, 9F, 71F, 159F, 233F, 313F, 387F,
463F, 537F, 599F, 649F, 701F
Grab-and-Go! Differentiated Centers Kit, In every Teacher Guide
lesson. Some examples are: 52, 202, 338, 618, 750
Quick Check, In every Teacher Edition lesson. Some examples
are: 32, 88, 280, 480, 610, 736
RtI Activities
RtI Tier 1 and RtI Tier 2 available online.
RtI Tier 3 Activities, 9I, 9, 159, 233F, 233, 313I, 313, 387,
463, 537, 599, 649A, 649, 701F, 701
Show What You Know, 10, 72, 160, 234, 314, 388, 464, 538,
600, 650, 702

Digital clocks, 510–512, 516–518, 521–524, 527–530

Digital Resources, *1C–1D, 9A–9C, 71A–71C, 151C–151D,*
159A–159D, 233A–233C, 313A–313D, 387A–387D,
455C–455D, 463A–463D, 537A–537C, 599A–599C,
649A–649C, 693C–693D, 701A–701D
See Technology and Digital Resources

Digits
defined, 9H, 25A, 26, 129A, 313H
lining up, 279A
values of, 25–28, 31–34, 37–39, 87–90, 93–96, 99–102,
111–113, 123–126, 279–282, 353–356

Dimes, *463H,* 467–470, 473–476, 479–482, 485–488, 491–493,
497–500, 503–506

Dividing, *753, 753A, 765A, 767*

Dollar, *463H, 491A,* 491–493, 497–500, 503–506

Dollar sign, *463H,* 492–493, 497–500, 503–506

Doubles and near doubles facts, *159E, 163A,* 163–166

Doubles minus one, *159E, 163A*

Doubles plus one, *159E, 163A*

Draw a Diagram strategy, 285–288, 365–368, *565A,*
565–567, *621A,* 621–623, 765–768

Edges, *701H,* 712–714

Elaborate, 15, 21, 27, 33, 39, 45, 57, 63, 76, 83, 89, 95, 101,
107, 119, 125, 131, 138, 143, 165, 171, 177, 189, 195,
207, 213, 225, 239, 245, 257, 263, 269, 275, 281, 288,
293, 299, 305, 319, 325, 331, 337, 343, 355, 361, 368,
373, 379, 393, 399, 405, 411, 417, 429, 435, 441, 447,
469, 475, 481, 487, 493, 499, 511, 517, 523, 529, 543,
549, 555, 561, 573, 579, 585, 591, 605, 611, 617, 629,
635, 641, 655, 661, 667, 673, 679, 686, 707, 713, 719,
725, 731, 737, 743, 749, 755, 761

ELL Language Support Strategies,
Cooperative Grouping, 99, 123, 279, 285, 313G, 323, 335, 347,
359, 377, 433, 485, 633, 677, 683, 747
Develop Meanings, 25, 193, 341, 553, 649G, 4781, 659, 671
Ellicit Prior Knowledge, 9G, 13, 31, 43, 55
Frontload, 71G, 75, 87, 117, 135
Identify Relationships, 37, 129, 187, 463G, 467, 491, 497, 515,
583, 765
Illustrate Understanding, 19, 93, 141, 163, 217, 261, 303, 329,
427, 503, 615, 665, 701G, 705, 723, 729, 735, 759
Model Concepts, 81, 159G, 169, 175, 181, 199, 211, 353, 365,
403, 421, 753
Model Language, 105, 223, 243, 537G, 562, 565, 571,
577, 589
Rephrase, 49, 317, 371, 473, 541, 599G, 603, 609, 621, 639
Restate, 255, 273, 387G, 397, 409, 439, 509, 521, 711
Scaffold Language, 61, 111, 233G, 237, 249, 267, 291, 297, 391,
415, 479, 547, 627, 717, 741
Understand Context, 205, 445, 527

End-of-Year Resources
End-of-Year Planner, PG40–PG41
End-of-Year Resources, PG38
Getting Ready for Grade 3 Lessons and Tests, PG50–PG93
Review Projects, PG44–PG49

Engage, *In every Teacher Edition lesson. Some examples are:*
19B, 199B, 329B, 473B, 583B, 711B

English Learners Language (ELL)
*Vocabulary Activity, 9H, 71H, 159H, 233H, 313H, 387H, 463H,
537H, 599H, 649H, 701H*

Enrich, *13, 19, 25, 31, 37, 43, 49, 55, 61, 75, 81, 87, 93, 99,
105, 111, 117, 123, 129, 135, 141, 163, 169, 175, 181, 187,
193, 199, 205, 211, 217, 223, 237, 243, 249, 255, 261, 267,
273, 279, 285, 291, 297, 303, 317, 323, 329, 335, 341, 347,
353, 359, 365, 371, 377, 391, 397, 403, 409, 415, 421, 427,
433, 439, 445, 467, 473, 479, 485, 491, 497, 503, 509, 515,
521, 527, 541, 547, 553, 559, 565, 571, 577, 583, 589, 603,
609, 615, 621, 627, 633, 639, 653, 659, 665, 671, 677, 683,
705, 711, 717, 723, 729, 735, 741, 747, 753, 759, 765*

Enrichment, *9, 159, 233, 313, 387, 463, 537, 599, 649, 701*

Equal, *747A*

Equal groups
in counting, *20A,* 20–22
problem solving for, *217A,* 217–220, *223A,* 223–226
repeated addition for, *187A,* 187–226

Equal parts of a whole, *217A, 747A,* 747–750, *753A,*
753–756, *759A,* 759–762, 765–768

Equal shares, *765A*

Errors, Common. *See Common Errors*; Mid-Chapter
Checkpoint

Essential Question, Chapter, *9A,* 67, *71A,* 147, *159A,* 229,
233A, 309, *313A,* 383, *387A,* 451, *463A,* 533, *537A,* 595,
599A, 645, *649A,* 689, *701A,* 771

Essential Question, Lesson
In every Student Edition lesson. Some examples are: 13,181, 329,
553, 671, 711
*In every Teacher Edition lesson. Some examples are: 13B, 205B,
353B, 497B, 547B, 759B*

Estimation
concept of, *553A,* 554, *599I*
defined, *633A*
of lengths in centimeters, *609A,* 609–612
of lengths in feet, *577A,* 577–580
of lengths in inches, *553A,* 553–556, *577A, 589*
of lengths in meters, *633A,* 633–636

Evaluate, 300, 306

Evaluate, *16, 22, 28, 34, 39, 46, 52, 58, 64, 78, 84, 90, 96,
108, 113, 120, 126, 132, 138, 144, 166, 172, 178, 184,
190, 195, 202, 208, 214, 220, 226, 240, 246, 252, 258,
264, 270, 275, 282, 288, 294, 300, 306, 320, 326, 332,
338, 344, 349, 356, 362, 368, 374, 380, 394, 400, 406,
412, 417, 424, 430, 442, 476, 482, 488, 493, 500, 506,
512, 518, 524, 530, 544, 550, 556, 562, 567, 574, 580,
586, 592, 606, 612, 618, 623, 630, 636, 642, 656, 662,
667, 674, 680, 686, 708, 714, 720, 726, 732, 738, 743,
750, 756, 762, 768*

Even numbers
defined, *9H, 11,* 14
model and classify, 13–16
represent as a sum of two equal addends, 19–22

Expanded form, 31–34, 37–40, 43–46, 93–96, 111–113

Explain, *14, 26, 32, 38, 44, 51, 56, 62, 76, 82, 88, 94, 100, 106,
112, 118, 124, 130, 137, 142, 164, 170, 176, 182, 189, 194,
200, 206, 212, 219, 224, 238, 244, 250, 256, 262, 268, 274,
280, 287, 292, 298, 304, 318, 324, 330, 336, 342, 348, 354,
360, 367, 372, 378, 392, 398, 404, 410, 416, 423, 428, 434,
440, 446, 468, 474, 480, 486, 492, 498, 505, 510, 516, 522,
524, 528, 542, 548,* 550, *554, 560, 567, 572, 574, 578, 584,
590, 592, 604, 610, 616, 628, 634, 640, 655, 660, 666, 668,
672, 674, 678, 718, 730, 742, 754*

Explain a Method, 344

Explore, *In every Teacher Edition lesson. Some examples are: 13,
93, 249, 583, 603, 683, 723, 753*
Listen and Draw appears in most Student Edition lessons. Some
examples are: 25, 49, 391, 415, 671, 753
Model and Draw appears in most Student Edition lessons. Some
examples are: 14, 164, 342, 542, 660, 736

Faces
defined, *701H,* 712
of three-dimensional shapes, 711–714

Facts. *See* Problem of the Day

Family Involvement
*School-Home Letter, 12, 74, 162, 236, 316, 390, 466, 540, 602,
652, 704*

Take Home Activity, 16, 22, 28, 34, 39, 46, 52, 58, 64, 78, 84, 90, 96, 102, 108, 113, 120, 126, 138, 144, 166, 172, 178, 184, 190, 195, 202, 208, 214, 220, 226, 240, 246, 252, 258, 264, 270, 275, 282, 288, 294, 300, 306, 320, 326, 332, 338, 344, 349, 356, 362, 368, 374, 380, 394, 400, 406, 412, 417, 424, 430, 436, 442, 448, 470, 476, 482, 488, 493, 500, 506, 512, 518, 524, 530, 544, 550, 556, 562, 574, 580, 586, 592, 606, 612, 618, 630, 636, 642, 656, 662, 667, 674, 680, 686, 708, 714, 720, 726, 732, 738, 743, 750, 756, 762, 768

Feet, 571–574, 577–580

Fewer than, 736

Figures. *See* Three-dimensional shapes; Two-dimensional shapes

Find a Pattern strategy, 49–52

Fluency
    addition and subtraction within 20, 163–166, 169–172, 175–178, 181–184, 187–190, 193–195, 199–202
    addition and subtraction within 100, 237–240, 243–246, 249–252, 255–258, 261–264, 267–270, 273–275, 279–282, 297–300, 303–306, 317–320, 323–326, 329–332, 335–338, 341–344, 347–349, 353–356, 359–362
    Math Story for, 151–158

Fluency Builder
    addition within 10, 55B
    basic facts, 223B, 243B, 279B, 329B, 353B, 377B, 409B, 497B, 583B, 677B, 741B, 759B
    breaking apart numbers to subtract, 365B
    counting numbers, 31B, 49B, 55B, 61B, 81B, 193B
    counting tape, 291B, 371B
    even or odd, 559B
    examples, 13B, 55B
    Mental Math, 129B, 237B, 285B, 427B, 439B, 445B, 565B, 621B, 765B
    modeling three-digit numbers, 87B
    place value, 93B, 479B, 547B, 609B
    quarter past, 521B
    related facts, 359B
    repeated addition, 697B
    three-digit addition, 485B, 609B
    time to the hour and half hour, 515B
    two-digit addition, 303B, 397B, 527B

Focus, in every Teacher Edition lesson. Some examples are: 61A, 141A, 181A,237A, 323A, 467, 571A, 701A

Foot, 537H, 571A

Formative Assessment, 40, 114, 196, 276, 350, 418, 494, 568, 624, 668, 744

For the Teacher, In Student Edition lessons. Some examples are: 13, 37, 359, 409, 633, 705

A fourth of, 759A, 760

Fourths, *701H, 747A, 747–750, 749, 753A, 753–756, 759–762, 765–768*

Fractions, foundation for, equal parts of a whole, *701E, 747A, 747–750, 753A, 753–756, 759A, 759–762, 765A, 765–768*

Frequency, *649E*

Games
    Caterpillar Chase, 162
    5 and 10 Count, 466
    Count the Sides, 704
    2-Digit Shuffle, 390
    Estimating Length, 602
    Fish for Digits, 74
    Longer or Shorter?, 540
    Making Tens, 652
    Subtraction Search, 316
    Three in a Row, 12
    What is the Sum?, 236

Games, Grab-and-Go Kit, In most Teacher Edition lessons. Some examples are: 16, 102, 202, 338, 602, 750

Games, Vocabulary. *See* Vocabulary Games

Geometry. *See* Shapes

Getting Ready for Grade 3 Lessons, PG50–PG93
    addition
        addition function tables, PG50–PG51
        estimating, 2-digit addition, PG52–PG53
        estimating, 3-digit addition, PG54–PG55
    algebra
        addition function tables, PG50–PG51
    Checkpoints, Getting Ready for Grade 3, PG61, PG73, PG85, PG91
    equal groups
        of 2, PG62–PG63
        of 3, PG64–PG65
        of 10, PG66–PG67
    equal shares
        number of, PG70–PG71
        size of, PG68–PG69
        solving problems with, PG72–PG73

fraction models
    comparing, *PG90–PG91*
    fourths and eighths, *PG88–PG89*
    thirds and sixths, *PG86–PG87*
measurement
    describing data, *PG84–PG85*
    nonstandard units, *PG82–PG83*
ordering, 3-digit numbers, *PG60–PG61*
subtraction
    estimating, 2-digit subtraction, *P56–P57*
    estimating, 3-digit subtraction, *P58–P59*
tables
    addition function tables, *PG50–PG51*
Test, Getting Ready for Grade 3, *PG74–PG75, PG92–PG93*
time
    elapsed, in hours, *PG78–PG79*
    elapsed, in minutes, *PG80–PG81*
    hour before and hour after, *PG76–PG77*

Glossary, H1–H10

Glossary, Multimedia. *See* Technology and Digital Resources

Go Deeper, *15, 21, 27, 33, 39, 45,* 46, *57, 63,* 77, *83, 89, 95,* 96, 101, *107, 113, 119, 125,* 126, *131,* 132, *137, 143, 165,* 166, *171,* 172, *177,* 178, *183, 189, 195, 201,* 202, 207, *213,* 214, *219, 225,* 226, *239,* 240, *245, 251, 257, 263, 269,* 270, *275, 281, 287,* 288, *293, 299, 305,* 306, *319,* 325, 331, *337, 343,* 349, *355,* 356, *361, 367,* 368, 373, *379,* 380, *393, 399,* 400, *405, 411,* 412, *423, 429, 435,* 441, 442, *447, 469, 475,* 481, 482, *487, 493, 499,* 500, *505, 511, 517, 523, 529,* 530, *543, 549, 555, 561, 573, 579, 585, 591, 605, 611, 617,* 629, *635, 641,* 655, 661, 662, 667, 673, *679,* 680, 686, *707,* 713, 714, *719,* 720, 725, *731, 737, 749, 755,* 756, *761, 767,* 768

Go Digital
    In every Student Edition lesson. Some examples are: 11, 161, 315, 465, 651, 703
    In every Teacher Edition lesson. Some examples are: *67H, 233F, 433B, 537F*

Go Math! and the Principles of Effective Mathematics Programs, *PG18–PG19*

Go Math! Program Overview. *See* Program Overview

Go Math! Sequence Options, *PG98–PG99*

Grab-and-Go!™ Differentiated Centers Kit, *In every Teacher Edition lesson. Some examples are: 16, 102, 202, 338, 602, 750*

Grab-and-Go™ Differentiated Centers Kit, Correlation, *PG94–PG97*

Graphic Organizers, *9H,* 11, 73, *159H,* 161, 235, *313H,* 315, 389, *463H,* 465, *537H,* 539, *599H,* 601, *649H,* 651, 703

Graphs and charts
    bar graphs
        defined, *649H,* 672
        making, *677A,* 677–680, *683A,* 683–686
        picture graphs compared with, *671A*
        reading, 671–674
        using to solve problems, 671–674, 677–680, 683–686
    labels on, 677A, 683A
    line plots, 589–592
    picture graphs, *653A, 659A, 683A*
        bar graphs compared with, *671A*
        defined, *649H,* 660
        making, 665–667
        reading, 659–662
        using to solve problems, 659–662, 665–667, 671
    tally charts, 653–656, 659, 666–667
    understanding information in, 649E, 659A
    using cubes, 665A

Greater than, *71H, 371A*

Greatest value, 479

A half of, *759A*

Halves, *701H, 747A,* 747–750, *753A,* 753–756, 759–762, *765A,* 765–768

Hands-On activities. *See* Activities

Hands-On lessons, 13–16, 87–90, 485–488, 541–544, 547–550, 559–562, 571–574, 603–606, 615–618, 627–630, 639–642, 741–743

Hexagons, *701H,* 723–726, *729A,* 730–731, *747*

HMH Mega Math, *In most Teacher Edition lessons. Some examples are: 81A, 267A, 377A, 553A, 753A*

Home Activity. *See* Family Involvement; Take Home Activity

Hour, 509–512, *509A,* 515–518, 521–524

Hour hand, *509A,* 509–512, 515–518, 521–524

Hundreds
    counting patterns with, 61–64, 123–126, 130–132
    defined, *71H, 75A,* 76, *387H*
    grouping tens as, 75–78
    hundreds chart, 10, *55A,* 55, 61
    model numbers to, *387I,* 388, *391A,* 392–393
    place value, 75–78, 81–84, 87–90, 93–96, 99–102, 105–108, 111–113, 117–120, 141–144, *273A*

If Children Ask, *37A, 55A, 193A, 243A, 273A, 285A, 353A, 377A, 421A, 445A, 527A, 553A, 615A, 697A, 747A*

Inches, *537H, 541–543, 547–550, 553–556, 559–562, 565–567, 571–574, 589–592*

Inch ruler, *584–586*

Independent Activities. *See under Activities*

Intensive Intervention, *9, 71, 159, 233, 313, 387, 463, 537, 599, 649, 701*

Interactive Student Edition, *In every Teacher Edition lesson. Some examples are: 31B, 129B, 323B, 467B, 571B, 717B*

Intervention
   Activities, Tier 1, available online for every lesson. See also Review Prerequisite Skills
   Activities, Tier 2, available online for every lesson.
   Activities, Tier 3, 9I, 9, 159, 233F, 233, 313I, 313, 387, 463, 537, 599, 649A, 649, 701F, 701
   Assessment, Diagnosis, Intervention, PG14
   Chapter At A Glance, 9A, 71A, 159A, 233A, 313A, 387A, 463A, 537A, 599A, 649A, 701A
   Daily Classroom Management, 9F, 71F, 159F, 233F, 313F, 387F, 463F, 537F, 599F, 649F, 701F
   Data-Driven Decision Making, 40, 67–68, 70A–70B, 114, 147–148, 150A–150B, 196, 229–230, 232A–232B, 276, 309–310, 312A–312B, 350, 383–384, 386A–386B, 418, 451–452, 454A–454B, 494, 533–534, 536A–536B, 568, 595–596, 598A–598B, 624, 645–646, 648A–648B, 668, 689–690, 692A–692B, 744, 771–772, 774A–774B
   Diagnostic Assessment, 10, 72, 160, 234, 314, 388, 464, 538, 600, 650, 702
   Enrich. See Enrich
   Intensive Intervention, 9, 71, 159, 233, 313, 387, 463, 537, 599, 649, 701
   On-Level Intervention, 9, 71, 159, 233, 313, 387, 463, 537, 599, 649, 701
   Options, 9, 71, 159, 233, 313, 387, 463, 537, 599, 649, 701
   Personal Math Trainer, In every Teacher Edition lesson. Some examples are: 10, 100, 276, 350, 494, 568, 668, 689
   Quick Check, In every Teacher Edition lesson. Some examples are: 26, 106, 194, 416, 548, 660, 754
   Reteach, 13, 19, 25, 31, 37, 43, 49, 55, 61, 75, 81, 87, 93, 99, 105, 111, 117, 123, 129, 135, 141, 163, 169, 175, 181, 187, 193, 199, 205, 211, 217, 223, 237, 243, 249, 255, 261, 267, 273, 279, 285, 291, 297, 303, 317, 323, 329, 335, 341, 347, 353, 359, 365, 371, 377, 391, 397, 403, 409, 415, 421, 427, 433, 439, 445, 467, 473, 479, 485, 491, 497, 503, 509, 515, 521, 527, 541, 547, 553, 559, 565, 571, 577, 583, 589, 603, 609, 615, 621, 627, 633, 639, 653, 659, 665, 671, 677, 683, 705, 711, 717, 723, 729, 735, 741, 747, 753, 759, 765

Review Prerequisite Skills, *9I, 71I, 159I, 233I, 313I, 387I, 463I, 537I, 599I, 649I, 701I*

Strategic Intervention, *9, 10, 71, 72, 159, 160, 233, 234, 313, 314, 387, 388, 463, 464, 537, 538, 599, 600, 649, 650, 701, 702*

Introduce the Chapter, *9, 71, 315, 377, 457, 463, 515, 537, 599, 649, 701*

Inverse relationship
   of addition and subtraction, *159E,* 187–190
   between size of units and number of units needed to measure, 571–574, 627–630

iTools, *In most Teacher Edition lessons. Some examples are: 19A, 329A, 415A, 527A, 621A, 735A*

Key, used in a picture graph, 659–662, 665–667, *671A,* 671

K.I.M. diagram, *159H, 313H, 599H*

Language, Developing Math, *9H, 71H, 159H, 233H, 313H, 387H, 463H, 537H, 599H, 649H, 701H*

Language Support, ELL, *See ELL Language Support Strategies*

Learning Objective, *In every Teacher Edition lesson. Some examples are: 13A, 37A, 615A, 753A*

Learning Progressions Across the Grades, *9J, 71J, 159J, 233J, 313J, 387J, 463J, 537J, 599J, 649H, 701J*

Least value, *479*

Length
   addition and subtraction of, 565–567, *621A,* 621–623
   in centimeters, 603–606, 609, 615–618, 627–630, 639–642
   choosing tools for measuring, 583–586
   comparing, *609A,* 609, 635, *639A,* 639–642
   data displayed in line plots, 589–592, 686
   estimation of, *553A,* 553–556, *577A,* 577–580, 609–612, 633–636
   in feet, 571–574, 577–580
   in inches, 541–544, 547–550, 553, 559–562, 565–567, 571–574, 589–592
   in meters, 627–630, 633–636
   in metric units, *599E, 615A, 633A, 639A*
   in nonstandard units, *603A*
   inverse relationship between size of units and number of units needed to measure, 571–574, 627–630

Lesson at a Glance, *In every Teacher Edition lesson. Some examples are: 13A, 255A, 329A, 427A, 521A, 639A, 741A*

Less than, *71H, 371A*

Line plots, *537H,* 589–592, 686

Listen and Draw In most Student Edition lessons. Some
examples are: 25, 49, 391, 415, 671, 753
Math Story, 1–8, 151–158, 455–462, 693–700

Literature
*Grab-and-Go!™ Differentiated Centers Kit, In most Teacher
Edition lessons. Some examples are: 13B, 16, 163B, 166, 349,
448, 556, 653B, 656*

Longer, *639A*

Make a Model strategy, 135–138, 421–424

Make Arguments, 15, 119, 435

Make a Ten, *159E,* 177

Make Connections, 34, 46, 189, 220, 246, 374, 476, 512, 708,
714, 738, 750

Manipulatives and Materials
addition fact cards, 181
base-ten blocks, *9E,* 31, *43A,* 43, *49, 71E, 76, 87A,* 87–90, *93A,
93, 99A,* 117, 131, *135A,* 135–138, 237, *255A,* 255, 261,
313E, 313H, 313I, 314, *317A,* 329, 335, *341A, 387I, 391A,
403A, 403, 409, 415, 421A,* 421–424, 427, *599A, 599H,
627, 633*
centimeter rulers, 615–618, 628–630, 639–642
clocks, analog, 463I, 509A, 509, 511, 515A, 515, 521A
color tiles, 193, *541A,* 541–543, 547, 548, *599I,* 600, 603, *741A,*
741–743
connecting cubes, *13, 19A, 43A,* 169, 365, *467,* 600, *649A, 649I,
650, 653, 653, 665A,* 665, *665, 697A, 718*
Counting Chart, 61
dot paper, 701A
fraction circles, 753, 755
fraction strips, 759
Hundred Chart, 10, 55, 61
inch rulers, 560–562, 572–574, 577–580, 584–585,
589–592
*index cards, 99A, 255A, 297A, 313H, 317A, 341A, 347A, 469,
475, 481, 729*
MathBoards, 19A, 50, *75A, 81A, 217A, 250, 273A, 329A, 365A,
378, 379, 415A, 463B, 537B, 599A, 633A, 649A, 649B,
697A, 701A–701D, 729A, 753A, 767*
Math Mountain Cards, 159I, 243A
measuring tape, *537H,* 584–586

Number Cubes, 652
Numeral Cards, 105A
paper plates, 747A
pattern blocks, 729, 735A, 735, 747
Place-Value Charts, 77
plane shapes, 765
play money, *463A–463B, 467A,* 467, 473, 479, 485–488,
503–506
poster board, 600
rulers, *547A, 559A, 571A, 599E,* 616, 639
Secret Code Cards, 99A, 111A, 111, 313I, 479A, 609A
Semantic Map, 9H, 67H, *537H*
Spinners, 379I, 466
Tangram Pattern, 725
Ten Frame, 175, *175A*
three-dimensional shapes, 723
two-color counters, *55A, 163,* 175, *181A, 217A,* 217,
223, 314
unit cubes, *603A, 603, 603, 615, 627A, 707,* 717–720
Venn diagram, 55A
Workmats, 233H, 255, 335
yardstick, *537H,* 583–586

Materials, Lesson. *See Chapter at a Glance; Lesson at a
Glance*

MathBoards, *19A, 75A, 81A, 217A, 250, 273A, 329A, 365A,
378, 379, 415A, 463B, 537B, 599A, 633A, 649A, 649B, 697A,
701A–701D, 729A, 753A,* 767

Math Journal. *See Writing, Math Journal*

Math on the Spot, 16, 21, 27, 33, 39, 45, 51, 63, 77, 83, 95,
120, 125, 144, 165, 166, 171, 177, 184, 190, 195, 201, 207,
213, 219, 226, 239, 245, 251, 257, 258, 263, 269, 275, 281,
287, 293, 299, 305, 319, 325, 332, 338, 343, 349, 355, 361,
367, 373, 380, 393, 399, 405, 412, 417, 423, 429, 436, 441,
447, 448, 469, 470, 475, 487, 493, 499, 505, 511, 518, 524,
529, 544, 550, 555, 562, 567, 574, 580, 586, 592, 606, 612,
618, 623, 630, 636, 641, 642, 656, 661, 667, 673, 679, 685,
686, 707, 713, 719, 726, 731, 737, 743, 749, 750, 756, 762,
767

Math Processes and Practices, *In every Teacher Edition
lesson. Some examples are: 90, 258, 380, 448, 606, 623, 706,
750*

Math Processes and Practices
1. *Problem Solving.* In many lessons. Some examples are: *58,
485A, 537E, 719*
2. *Abstract and Quantitative Reasoning.* In many lessons. Some
examples are: *9E, 211A, 233E*
3. *Use and Evaluate Logical Reasoning.* In many lessons. Some
examples are: *19, 43, 55, 347, 463E, 171*

4. *Mathematical Modeling.* In many lessons. Some examples are: *13, 19, 25, 31, 33, 55, 58, 300, 313E, 488, 621A, 683A, 717, 765A*

5. *Use Mathematical Tools.* In many lessons. Some examples are: *359A, 403A, 538A, 593A, 701E*

6. *Use Precise Mathematical Language.* In many lessons. Some examples are: *25, 27, 37, 46, 50, 159E*

7. *See Structure.* In many lessons. Some examples are: *13,15, 21, 39, 43, 49, 57, 61A, 71E, 303A, 387E, 720*

8. *Generalize.* In many lessons. Some examples are: *19, 141A, 599E, 649E*

Building Math Processes and Practices, *61A, 141A, 303A, 359A, 383A, 403A, 485A, 583A, 621A, 683A, 765A*

Math Processes and Practices, *PG20–PG22*

Math Processes and Practices in Go Math! *PG24*

Supporting Math Processes and Practices Through Questioning Strategies, *PG23*

Math Story, 1–8, 151–158, 455–461, 693–700

Math Talk, In every Student Edition lesson. Some examples are: 13, 163, 341, 553, 659, 735

Measurable attributes, *527E*

Measurement
  building understanding of, 537E
  in centimeters, 603–606, 609, 615–618, 627–630, 639–642
  choosing tools for, *583A,* 583–586, *639A*
  with color tiles, 541A
  in feet, 571–574, 591–596
  in inches, 541–544, 547–550, 553, 559–562, 565–567, 571–574, 589–592
  in meters, 627–630, 633–636
  in nonstandard units, 541A, 603A
  with unit cubes, 603A
  units of, *599E,* 603–606, *615A, 627A,* 627–630, *633A*

Mega Math, HMH. *See* Technology and Digital Resources

Meters, *599H, 627A,* 627–630, 633–636, *639A*

Meter sticks, *627A,* 629

Metric units, *599E, 615A, 633A*

Mid-Chapter Checkpoint, 40, 114, 196, 276, 350, 418, 494, 568, 624, 668, 744

Midnight, *463H,* 528

Minutes, *463H,* 510–512, 515–518, 521–524

Minute hand, 510–512

Mixed numbers, *497A*

Model
  addition
    make a ten to add, 159E, 177, 233E
    two-digit, 261–264

bar graphs, *415A, 649H, 671A,* 671–674, 677–680, *683A,* 683–686

bar models, *187A,* 187–188, *205A,* 205–208, *285A,* 285–288, 291, *365A,* 365–368, 377–380

in classifying, 13–16

fractions, 765A

make a model strategy, 135–138, 421–424

number lines, 318, *359A,*

numbers in different ways, *43A,* 111–113, 117–120

regrouping
  for addition, 255–258
  for subtraction, 329–332, *433A, 439A*

subtraction, *313E*
  bar models, 205A, *365A,* 365
  regrouping for, 329–332, *433A, 439A*
  three-digit, 421–424
  two-digit, 335–338, 341

three-digit numbers, 87–90

using, 470, 517

Model and Draw, *14, 20, 26, 32, 38, 44, 56, 62, 76, 82, 88, 94, 100, 106, 112, 118, 124, 130, 142, 164, 170, 176, 182, 188, 194, 200, 206, 212, 224, 238, 244, 250, 256, 262, 268, 274, 280, 292, 298, 304, 318, 324, 330, 336, 342, 348, 354, 360, 372, 378, 392, 398, 404, 410, 416, 428, 434, 440, 446, 468, 474, 480, 486, 492, 498, 510, 516, 522, 528, 542, 548, 554, 560, 572, 578, 584, 590, 604, 610, 616, 628, 634, 640, 654, 660, 666, 672, 678, 706, 712, 718, 724, 730, 736, 742, 748, 754, 760*

Models
  Using Bar Models, 187A
  Using Base-Ten Blocks to Compare, 135A
  Using Color Tiles to Measure Length, 541A
  Using Number Sentences, 211A
  Using Pattern Blocks, 735A
  Using Quick Pictures, 273A, 421A, 521A
  Using Secret Code Cards, 111A
  Using a Ten Frame, 175A
  Using Three-Dimensional Models, 705A
  Using Unit Cubes to Measure Length, 603A

Money
  cent sign, 467–470, 473–476, 479–482, 485–488, 491, 497
  coins
    counting collections, 467–470, 473–476, 479–482
    dimes, 467–470, 473–476, 479–482, 485–488, 491–493, 497–500, 503–506
    nickels, 467–470, 473–476, 479–482, 485–488, 491–493, 497–500, 503–506
    pennies, 467–470, 473–476, 479–482, 485–488, 491–493, 497–500, 503–506
    quarters, 473–476, 479–482, 485–488, 492–493, 497–500

counting, *463A, 463E, 467A, 467–470, 473A, 479A, 479–482,*
485A, 485–488, *491A, 499, 503A*
decimal notation for, 463E, 497A, 499, 503A
dollars, 491–493, 497–500, 503–506
dollar sign, 492–493, 497–500, 503–506

More than, 736

Most Difficult 2-Digit Addition Problem, 274

Multimedia eGlossary, 9H, 71H, 159H, 233H, 313H, 387H,
463H, 537H, 599H, 649H, 701H

Multistep problems, 126, 131, 184, 190, 214, 258, 288, 293,
319, *377A,* 377–380, 405, 412, *424,* 436, 679, 680

My Math/Project Storybook, 158B, 462B, 700B

Nickels, *463H,* 467–470, 473–476, 479–482, 485–488, 491–493,
497–500, 503–506

Noon, *463H,* 528, 530

Number line diagrams, 565–567, 621–623

Number lines, 199–201, 318–319, 323–325, 360–362, 374,
565–567, 621–623

Number of the Day. See Problem of the Day

Number patterns, 49–52, 55–58, 61–64, 129–132, 195

Numbers
classifying as even or odd, 13–16
comparing, 135–138, 141–144
concepts, 9E
different forms of, 111–113
different ways to show, 37–40, 43–46, 105–108, 111–113,
117–120
expanded form, 31–34, 37–39, 93–96, 111–113, *117A, 249A*
in patterns, 49–52, 55–58, 61–64, 129–132, 195
place value in, 25–28, 81–84, 87–90, 93–96, 99–102, 105–108,
111–113, 117–120, 123–126
word form, 38–39, 105–108, 111–113

Number sentences, 211A, 291A

Odd numbers, *9H, 11,* 13–16, 19, 21

Ones, 313H, 317A

On-Level Intervention. See Intervention

Online Assessment Guide. See Technology and Digital Resources

On Your Own, In every Student Edition lesson. Some examples
are: 15, 183, 349, 549, 673, 737

Order of addends, *169A,* 169–172, *181A,* 181–184, 297–300,
303–306

Partitioning shapes, 741–743, 747–750, 753–756, 759–762,
765–768

Part-whole relationship
addition, 31A
bar models, 187A, 187, 285A, 285
fractions and, 701E
model, 31A
subtraction, 159E

Patterns. *See Counting Patterns*

Pennies, *463H,* 467–470, 473–476, 479–482, 485–488,
491–493, 497–500, 503–506

Pentagons, *701H,* 723–726, *729A,* 730–732, 736, 738

Personal Math Trainer, 10, 22, 52, 72, 102, 144, 160, 172, 214,
234, 252, 264, 314, 332, 344, 388, 394, 430, 436, 464, 476,
500, 538, 544, 586, 606, 642, 650, 680, 686, 702, 720, 750
Also in every Teacher Edition lesson. Some examples include: 10,
100, 276, 350, 494, 568, 668, 689

Picture Glossary, PG100–PG102

Picture graphs
defined, *649H,* 660
making, 665–667
reading, *659A,* 659–662
using to solve problems, 659–662, *665A,* 665–667, *671A,* 671

Place value
comparing numbers using, *135A,* 141–144
and counting patterns, 123–126, 129–132
2-digit numbers, *9E,* 25–28, 31–34, 37–39, 43–46
3-digit numbers, 75–78, 81–84, 87–90, 93–96, *93A, 99A,*
99–102, 105–108, 111–113, 117–120, 123–126, *397A*
in estimation, 141–144

Plane shape, 701E, 724, 765

Planning Resources
End-of-Year Planners, PG40–PG41
Year-At-A-Glance, PG30–PG37

p.m., *463H, 527A,* 527–530

Print Resources, *9A–9C, 71A–71C, 159A–159D, 233A–233B, 313A–313D, 387A–387D, 463A–463D, 537A–537C, 537A–537C, 599A–599C, 649A–649C, 701A–701D*

Problem of the Day

Basic Facts, 205B, 211B, 273B, 291B, 329B, 347B, 365B, 377B, 391B, 415B, 427B, 503B, 553B, 559B, 565B, 577B, 615B, 627B, 659B, 753

Calendar Math, 13B, 25B, 37B, 55B, 81B, 93B, 111B, 193B, 237B, 285B, 297B, 303B, 323B, 335B, 353B, 433B, 445B, 467B, 485B, 603B, 697B

Number of the Day, 19B, 31B, 43B, 49B, 61B, 75B, 87B, 117B, 123B, 163B, 169B, 181B, 187B, 217B, 243B, 249B, 255B, 261B, 279B, 317B, 341B, 359B, 371B, 397B, 409B, 421B, 439B, 463B, 491B, 497B, 509B, 521B, 541B, 571B, 589B, 609B, 621B, 653B, 665B, 671B, 683B, 697B, 705B, 729B, 735B, 759B, 765B

Secret Code Cards, 99B

Word of the Day, 105B, 129B, 135B, 223B, 267B, 403B, 479B, 515B, 527B, 547B, 583B, 633B, 639B, 677B, 741B, 747B

Problem Solving

Lessons, *49–52, 135–138, 217–220, 285–288, 365–368, 421–424, 503–506, 565–568, 621–624, 683–686, 765–768*

Multistep problems, *131, 184, 190, 214, 288, 293, 319, 377–380, 399, 405, 412, 436, 679, 680*

Real World Applications, In every Student Edition lesson. Some examples are: *22, 49, 58, 64, 78, 84, 102, 108, 120*

Unlock the problem, *49, 135, 217, 285, 365, 421, 503, 565, 621, 683, 765*

See also Problem Types, for word problems

Problem Solving, *In every Teacher Edition lesson. Some examples are: 16, 214, 400, 442, 618, 680, 756*

Problem-Solving Strategies

act it out, *217–220, 503–506*

breaking apart numbers, *317A, 323A, 325, 347A, 365A, 439A*

compensation, *243A*

concrete models, *439A*

count on, *159E*

doubles, *159E, 163A*

doubles minus one, *159E, 163A*

doubles plus one, *159E, 159E, 163A*

draw a diagram, *285–288, 365–368, 565–567, 621–623, 765–768*

find a pattern, *49–52*

invented strategies, *313E, 347*

make a graph, *683–686*

make a model, *135–138, 421–424*

part-part-whole relations, *159E*

pictorial models, *439A*

regrouping, *233H, 255A, 255–258, 261A, 261–264, 267A, 267–270, 273–275, 280–282, 297–300, 303–306, 313E, 313H, 313I, 329–332, 335–338, 341–344, 347–349, 353A, 353–356, 387H, 403A, 403–406, 409A, 409–412, 415A, 415–417, 427–430, 433A, 433–436, 439A, 439–442, 445A, 445–448*

think addition to subtract, *159E, 193A, 313E, 439A*

using known subtraction problems in, *347A*

Problem Types, for word problems

Add to

Change unknown, *285, 378*

Result unknown, *153, 154, 163, 172, 178, 184, 214, 230, 237, 243, 252, 264, 270, 279, 286–288, 291, 300, 306, 310, 320, 326, 359, 368, 377, 379–380, 391, 623, 674*

Start unknown, *213, 293*

Compare

Bigger unknown, *258, 343, 362, 406, 642*

Difference unknown, *190, 202, 206–208, 214, 231, 232, 326, 338, 356, 366–367, 372, 384–386, 412, 423, 439, 648, 654–656, 659–662, 672, 674, 680*

Smaller unknown, *332, 368, 448, 612*

Put Together/Take Apart

Addend unknown, *155, 184, 208, 212–213, 232, 252, 286–287, 292, 332, 347, 367, 374, 385–386, 422, 430, 433, 442, 448, 692*

Both Addends unknown, *246, 264, 282, 311, 380, 448, 606, 662, 768*

Total unknown, *152, 156, 166, 169, 175, 178, 184, 187, 190, 193, 196, 205, 207–208, 212–214, 230, 233, 237, 240, 246, 252, 255, 258, 261, 264, 267, 273–274, 276, 282, 287–288, 297, 300, 303, 306, 310–312, 326, 356, 377, 379, 385, 387, 394, 400, 403, 406, 409, 412, 415, 418, 434–436, 452, 566–567, 595, 598, 622, 636, 655–656, 661–662, 671–674, 677, 680, 692*

Take from

Change unknown, *187, 213, 320, 326, 371, 373, 427, 430*

Result unknown, *159, 187, 190, 199, 205–207, 212, 229, 313, 320, 323, 329, 332, 335, 338, 341, 344, 348, 350, 353, 359, 362, 365, 367–368, 372, 379, 384–386, 394, 421, 423–424, 430, 433, 436, 445–446, 453, 565–567, 621–623, 642*

Start unknown, *338, 373, 424*

Professional Development

About the Math

If Children Ask, *37A, 193A, 243A, 273A, 285A, 353A, 377A, 421A, 445A, 527A, 553A, 615A, 697A, 747A*

Teaching for Depth, *13A, 19A, 55A, 75A, 117A, 123A, 159E, 223A, 249A, 267A, 297A, 317A, 323A, 329A, 347A, 391A, 397A, 409A, 415A, 427A, 439A, 463A, 463E, 467A, 491A, 497A, 503A, 515A, 559A, 571A, 589A, 599E, 627A, 633A, 671A, 677A, 753A, 759A*

Why Teach This, *25A, 31A, 49A, 87A, 99A, 163A, 169A, 181A, 237A, 255A, 279A, 291A, 341A, 365A, 371A, 479A, 521A, 547A, 565A, 577A, 609A, 639A, 653A, 659A, 697A, 729A, 741A*

Building Math Processes and Practices, 61A, 141A, 303A, 359A, 383A, 403A, 485A, 583A, 621A, 683A, 765A

Math Processes and Practices, PG20

Professional Development Video, In each chapter and most Teacher Edition lessons. Some examples are: 13A, 163A, 479A, 615A, 701E, 753A

Supporting Math Processes and Practices Through Questioning Strategies, PG23

Professional Development References, *PG104–PG105*

Program Overview

About Go Math!, PG4

Assessment, Diagnosis, Intervention, PG14

Authors, Consultants, and Advisory Board, PG16–PG17

Go Math! and the Principles of Effective Mathematics Programs, *PG18–PG19*

Math Processes and Practices, PG20

Math Processes and Practices in Go Math!, PG24

Supporting Math Processes and Practices Through Questioning Strategies, PG23

Projects, *158B, 462B, 700B*

Properties of Addition

add in any order, *169A*, 169–172, *181A*

adding zero, 170–171

grouping addends in different ways, 181–184, 297–300, 303–306

Quadrilaterals, *701H*, 723–726, *729A*, 730–732, 735–738, 741–743

Quarter of, *759A, 760, 761*

Quarter past, *463H, 522*

Quarters, *463H*, 473–476, 479–482, 485–488, 492–493, 497–500

Quick Check, *In every Teacher Edition lesson. Some examples are: 32, 88, 410, 528, 666, 742*

Quick Pictures, 27, 32–33, 49, 87–89, 93, 99, 112–113, 117, 123, 135–138, 141, 238, 243, 255–258, 261–264, 267, *273A*, 309–310, 329, 335–338, 341, *348, 391A*, 391–394, 397, 403, 409, 415, *421A, 422*, 427, *429*, 433, *439*

Reading

Developing Math Language, 9H, 71H, 159H, 233H, 313H, 387H, 463H, 537H, 599H, 649H, 701H

Grab-and-Go!™ Differentiated Centers Kit, In most Teacher Edition lessons. Some examples are: 34, 202, 349, 448, 556, 726, 750

Vocabulary Story, 1–8, 150–151–158, 455–462, 693–700

Real World

Explore, 25, 31, 37, 43, 75, 81, 87, 93, 99, 111, 117, 123, 129, 141, 163, 169, 175, 187, 193, 199, 205, 211, 223, 237, 243, 255, 261, 267, 273, 279, 291, 297, 303, 323, 329, 335, 341, 347, 353, 359, 371, 377, 391, 403, 409, 415, 427, 433, 439, 445, 467, 473, 479, 485, 491, 497, 509, 515, 521, 541, 547, 553, 559, 577, 583, 589, 603, 609, 615, 627, 633, 639, 659, 671, 677, 705, 717

Problem Solving Applications, 22, 34, 46, 49, 58, 64, 78, 84, 96, 102, 108, 120, 126, 132, 144, 172, 178, 208, 214, 226, 246, 252, 258, 264, 270, 282, 294, 300, 306, 320, 326, 332, 338, 344, 356, 362, 374, 380, 394, 400, 406, 412, 430, 436, 442, 448, 470, 476, 482, 488, 500, 512, 518, 524, 530, 544, 550, 556, 562, 574, 580, 586, 592, 606, 612, 618, 630, 636, 642, 656, 662, 674, 680, 686, 708, 714, 720, 726, 732, 756

Unlock the Problem, 49, 135, 217, 285, 365, 421, 503, 565, 621, 683, 765

Rectangles

angles in, 729, 736–738

equal parts of, 748–750, 753–756, 759–762, 765–768

partition into rows and columns, *741A*, 741–743

Rectangular prisms

building, 718–720

defined, 701H

faces, edges, and vertices, 711–714, 718–720

identify and describe, 705–708, 717

References, Professional Development, *PG104–PG105*

Regrouping

in addition, 255A, 255–258, *261A*, 261–264, *267A*, 267–270, 273–275, 280–282, 297–300, 303–306, 403–406, *409A*, 409–412, *415A*, 415–417

comparing, in addition and subtraction, 337

defined, 233H, 313H, 387H

modeling, 313E, 313I

in subtraction, 329–332, 335–338, 341–344, 347–349, *353A*, 353–356, 427–430, *433A*, 433–436, *439A*, 439–442, *445A*, 445–448

Related facts, 187–190, *359A*

Resources. *See Chapter at a Glance; End-of-Year Resources; Planning Resources; Technology and Digital Resources*

Response to Intervention (RtI)
  Activities, Tier 3, 9I, 9, 159, 233F, 233, 313I, 313, 387, 463, 537, 599, 649A, 649, 701F, 701
  Chapter at a Glance, 9A, 71A, 151D, 159A, 233A, 313A, 387A, 455D, 463A, 537A, 599A, 649A, 649C, 701A
  Data-Driven Decision Making. See Data-Driven Decision Making
  Enrich. See Enrich
  Intervention Options, 9, 71, 159, 233, 313, 387, 463, 537, 599, 649, 701
  Reteach, 13, 19, 25, 31, 37, 43, 49, 55, 61, 75, 81, 87, 93, 99, 105, 111, 117, 123, 129, 135, 141, 163, 169, 175, 181, 187, 193, 199, 205, 211, 217, 223, 237, 243, 249, 255, 261, 267, 273, 279, 285, 291, 297, 303, 317, 323, 329, 335, 341, 347, 353, 359, 365, 371, 377, 391, 397, 403, 409, 415, 421, 427, 433, 439, 445, 467, 473, 479, 485, 491, 497, 503, 509, 515, 521, 527, 541, 547, 553, 559, 565, 571, 577, 583, 589, 603, 609, 615, 621, 627, 633, 639, 653, 659, 665, 671, 677, 683, 705, 711, 717, 723, 729, 735, 741, 747, 753, 759, 765
  Review Prerequisite Skills, 9I, 71I, 159I, 233I, 313I, 387I, 463I, 537I, 599I, 649I, 701I

Review Projects, *PG44–PG49*

Rhombus, *735*

Rigor, *In every Teacher Edition lesson. Some examples are: 61A, 141A, 181A, 237A, 323A, 467, 571A, 701A*

RtI. *See Response to Intervention (RtI)*

Scaffolding, *341A*

Scale, *on bar graphs, 671A, 677A*

Science, Connections to, *158A, 462A*

Sequence Options, Go Math! *PG98–PG99*

Shapes
  three-dimensional
    attributes of, 711–714
    building, 717–720
    identify and describe, *705A*, 705–708
  two-dimensional
    angles in, *701H*, 729–732, 736–738
    attributes of, *701E, 701I*, 723–726, 729–732, 735–738, *741*
    concepts, *701E*, 724

  equal parts of, *747A*, 747–750, *753A*, 753–756, 754, 755, *759A*, 759–762, 765–768
  identify and describe, 723–726
  partitioned into equal parts, 741–743, 747–750, 753–756, 759–762, 765–768
  pattern blocks for, 735A

Share and Show, *In every Student Edition lesson. Some examples are: 14, 170, 330, 542, 654, 736*

Shorter, *639A, 641*

Show What You Know, 10, 72, 160, 234, 314, 388, 464, 538, 600, 650, 702

Sides, *697A, 701H*, 723–726, 729–732, 735–738

Skip counting. *See Counting*

Small Group Options, *9F, 71F, 159F, 233F, 313F, 387F, 463F, 537F, 599F, 649F, 701F*

Social Studies, Connections to, *8A, 700A*

Solid figures, solid shapes. *See Three-dimensional shapes*

Sorting
  by attributes, 649I
  three-dimensional shapes, 705–708
  two-dimensional shapes, 723–726

Spheres, 705–708, 711, 717

Spiral Review, *In every Teacher Edition lesson. Some examples are: 55,199, 323, 347, 653*

Springboard to Learning, *In every Teacher Edition lesson. Some examples are: 20, 378, 554, 622, 748*

Squares, 711–714, 723–726, 735–738

Story problems, *291A, 371A*

Strategic Intervention. *See Intervention*

Strategies. *See Problem-Solving Strategies*

Student Edition, Interactive, *In every Teacher Edition lesson. Some examples are: 31B, 129B, 323B, 467B, 571B, 717B*

Student Edition Glossary, H1–H10

Subtraction
  basic facts, 187–190, 193–195, 199–202, 205–208, 211–214
  to compare, 205A
  concepts, 159E
  decomposing, 323A
  kinds of questions answered using, 366
  of lengths, 621A, 621–623
  mental math, 355

model
    bar models, 187–188, *205A*, 205–207, 211, *365A*, 365–368, 377–380, *379*
    number lines, 318, *359A*
regrouping in, 329–332, 335–338, 341–344, 347–349, *353A*, 353–356, *387E*, 421–424, 427–430, *433A*, 433–436, *439A*, 439–442, *445A*, 445–448
relate to addition, 187–190
scaffolding in, 341A
standard algorithm for, 335A, 347A, 427A, 433A, 439A, 445A
strategies
    breaking apart numbers, *317A*, 317–320, *323A*, 323–326, *347A, 365A, 439A*
    concrete models, *439A*
    part-part-whole relations, *159E*
    pictorial models, *439A*
    regroup, *233H*
    think addition to subtract, *159E, 193A, 313E, 439A*
    thinking of new, *347*
    using known subtraction problems in, *347A*
three-digit numbers
    regrouping concept with, *421A*, 421–424
    regroup both hundreds and tens, 439–442
    regroup hundreds, 433–436
    regroup tens, 427–430
    regrouping with zeros, 445–448
two-digit numbers
    adding to find differences, *359A*, 359–362
    breaking apart, *317A*, 317–320, *323A*, 323–326
    modeling regrouping for, *329A*, 329–332, *335A*, 335–338, 365–368
    multistep problems, *377A*, 377–380
    rewriting in vertical format, *353A*, 353–356
    solving, *341A*, 341–344, *347A*, 347–349
    writing equations for, *371A*, 371–374
using models and quick pictures, 329–332, 335–338, 341, 421–424, 427, 433, 439
using number lines, 199–201, 318–319, 323–325, 360–362
write equations to represent problems, 205–208, 211–214, 359, 365–368, 371–374
zero in, *348*, 445–448
See also Problem Solving; Problem Types

Subtrahends, *317A, 323A*

Sum, *159H, 267A, 387H*

Summarize, *424, 470*

Summative Assessment, *67–70, 70A–70B, 147–150, 150A–150B, 229–232, 232A–232B, 309–312, 312A–312B, 383–386, 386A–386B, 451–454, 454A–454B, 533–536, 536A–536B, 595–598, 598A–598B, 645–648, 648A–648B, 689–692, 692A–692B, 771–774, 774A–774B*

Supporting Math Processes and Practices Through Questioning Strategies, *PG23*

Surfaces, *717*

Surveys, *649H, 653A*, 653–656, *677A*

Symbols used in mathematics, 142–144

Symmetry, *697A*

Take Home Activity, 16, 22, 28, 34, 39, 46, 52, 58, 64, 78, 84, 90, 96, 102, 108, 113, 120, 126, 138, 144, 166, 172, 178, 184, 190, 195, 202, 208, 214, 220, 226, 240, 246, 252, 258, 270, 275, 282, 288, 294, 300, 306, 320, 326, 332, 338, 344, 349, 356, 362, 368, 374, 380, 394, 400, 406, 412, 417, 424, 430, 436, 442, 448, 470, 476, 482, 488, 493, 500, 506, 512, 518, 524, 530, 544, 550, 556, 562, 574, 580, 586, 592, 606, 612, 618, 630, 636, 642, 656, 662, 667, 674, 680, 686, 708, 714, 720, 726, 732, 738, 743, 750, 756, 762, 768

Tally charts, *653A*, 653–656, 659, 666–667, *679*

Tally marks, *653A, 683A*

Teacher Edition, Online. *See Chapter at a Glance*

Teaching for Depth
    About the Math, 13A, 19A, 55A, 75A, 117A, 123A, 159E, 223A, 249A, 267A, 297A, 317A, 323A, 329A, 347A, 391A, 397A, 409A, 415A, 427A, 439A, 463A, 463E, 467A, 491A, 497A, 503A, 515A, 559A, 571A, 589A, 599E, 627A, 633A, 671A, 677A, 753A, 759A
    Abstract and Quantitative Reasoning, 233E
    Addition Concepts, 9E, 249A
    Addition Strategies, 159E, 233E
    Building Understanding in Measurement, 537E
    Compare Numbers, 71E
    Counting Money, 463E
    Decimal System, 71E
    Decision Making Based on Data, 649E
    Errors in Measuring Length, 537E
    Foundation for Addition and Subtraction, 387E
    Importance of 10, 233E, 387E

Model with Mathematics, *313E*

Number Concepts, *9E*

Place Value, *9E, 71E, 397A*

Reasoning with Shapes and Fractions, *701E*

Reasoning with Shapes and Their Attributes, *701E*

Rulers, *559A*

Telling Time, *463E*

Understanding Numbers, *9E*

Understanding Value and Frequency, *649E*

Technology and Digital Resources

Animated Math Models, *In most Teacher Edition lessons. Some examples are: 13, 99, 255, 415, 615, 693, 705*

Chapter eResources, *Access through the Go Math! Online Planning Guide*

Digital Resources, *1C–1D, 9A–9C, 71A–71C, 151C–151D, 159A–159D, 233A–233C, 313A–313D, 387A–387D, 455C–455D, 463A–463D, 537A–537C, 599A*

eTeacher Resources

HMH Mega Math, *In most Teacher Edition lessons. Some examples are: 81A, 267A, 377A, 553A, 753A*

Interactive Student Edition, *In every Teacher Edition lesson. Some examples are: 31B, 129B, 323B, 467B, 571B, 717B*

iTools, *In most Teacher Edition lessons. Some examples are: 19A, 329A, 415A, 527A, 621A, 735A, 75A*

Multimedia eGlossary, *9H, 71H, 159H, 233H, 313H, 387H, 463H, 537H, 599H, 649H, 701H*

Personal Math Trainer, 476, 544, 606, 680, 720

    Also in every Teacher Edition lesson. Some examples include: *10, 100, 276, 350, 494, 568, 668, 689, 100, 276, 350, 494, 568, 600, 668, 689–690*

Professional Development Video, *In each chapter and most Teacher Edition lessons. Some examples are: 13A, 163A, 479A, 615A, 701E, 753A*

Tens, *313H, 409A*

Test Prep

Chapter Review/Test, 67–70, 147–150, 229–232, 309–312, 383–386, 451–454, 533–536, 595–598, 645–648, 689–692, 771–774

Mid-Chapter Checkpoint, 40, 114, 196, 276, 350, 418, 494, 568, 624, 668, 744

Think Smarter

Chapter Review/Test, 67–70, 147–150, 229–232, 309–312, 383–386, 451–454, 533–536, 595–598, 645–648, 689–692, 771–774

Mid-Chapter Checkpoint, 40, 114, 196, 276, 350, 418, 494, 568, 624, 668, 744

Think Smarter, 16, 21, 22, 27, 28, 33, 34, 39, 40, 45, 46, 51, 52, 57, 58, 63, 64, 77, 78, 83, 84, 90, 95, 96, 102, 107, 108, 113, 120, 125, 126, 131, 132, 138, 144, 165, 166, 171, 172, 177, 178, 184, 190, 195, 201, 202, 207, 213, 214, 219, 220, 226, 239, 240, 245, 246, 251, 257, 258, 263, 264, 269, 270, 275, 276, 281, 282, 287, 288, 293, 294, 299, 300, 305, 306, 319, 320, 325, 326, 332, 338, 343, 344, 349, 350, 355, 356, 361, 362, 367, 368, 373, 374, 380, 393, 394, 399, 400, 405, 406, 412, 417, 423, 424, 429, 430, 436, 441, 442, 447, 448, 469, 470, 475, 476, 482, 487, 488, 493, 499, 500, 505, 506, 511, 512, 518, 524, 529, 530, 544, 550, 555, 556, 562, 567, 574, 580, 586, 592, 606, 612, 618, 623, 630, 636, 641, 642, 656, 661, 662, 667, 673, 674, 679, 680, 685, 686, 707, 708, 713, 714, 719, 720, 726, 731, 732, 737, 738, 743, 744, 749, 750, 756, 762, 767, 768

A third of, *759A*

Thirds, *701H, 747A, 747–750, 753A, 753–756, 759–762, 765–768*

Thousand, *71H, 99–102*

Three-digit Addition, *398*

Three-digit numbers

addition, *391A, 391–394, 397A, 397–400, 403A, 403–406, 409A, 409–412, 415A, 415–417*

comparing, 135–138, 141–144

composing and decomposing, 117–120

counting patterns with, 61–64, 123–126, 129–132

different forms of, 111–113

expanded form, 93–96, 111–113

place value, 81–84, 87–90, 93–96, 99–102, 111–113, 123–126, 141–144

subtraction, *421A, 421–424, 427A, 427–430, 433A, 433–436, 439A, 439–442, 445A, 445–448*

using quick pictures to represent, 87–89, 93, 99, 117, 123, 391–394, 397, 403, 409, 415, 421–424, 427, 433, 439

word form, 105–108, 111–113

Three-dimensional shapes

attributes of, *701E, 711A, 711–714*

building, *717A, 717–720*

identify and describe, 693–696, *705A, 705–708*

Tier 1 Activities (RtI) are available online.

Tier 2 Activities (RtI) are available online.

Tier 3 Activities (RtI), *9I, 9, 159, 233F, 233, 313I, 313, 387, 463, 537, 599, 649A, 649, 701F, 701*

Time

a.m. and p.m., 527–530

clocks

analog, 509–512, 515–518, 521–524, 527–530

digital, 510–512, 516–518, 521–523, 527–529

to the hour and half hour, 515A

noon and midnight, 528

telling time, *463E, 509A,* 509–512, *515A,* 515–518, 521–524, *521A, 527A*

units of, *741A*

Trapezoid, *735*

Triangles, 723–726, *729A,* 729–732, 735–738, 749–750, 753

Try Another Problem, 50, 136, 218, 286, 366, 422, 504, 566, 622, 684, 766

Two-digit numbers

addition, 237–240, 243–246, 249–252, 255–258, 261–264, *267A,* 267–270, 273–275, 279–282, 285–288, 291–294, *297A,* 297–300, 303–306

composing and decomposing, 43–46, 49–52

counting patterns with, 55–58

different ways to represent, 31–34, 37–39, 43–46, 49–52

expanded form, 31–34

place value, 25–28, 31–34, 37–40, 43–46, *93A*

subtraction, 317–320, 323–326, 329–332, 335–338, 341–344, 347–349, 353–356, 359–362, 365–368, 371–374, 377–380

word form, 37–39

Two-dimensional shapes

angles in, 729–732, 736–738

attributes of, *701E,* 723–726, 729–732, 735–738, *741*

concepts, *701E, 724*

equal parts of, *747A,* 747–750, *753A,* 753, 754, 755, 756, *759A,* 759–762, 765–768

pattern blocks for, 735A

Understand Vocabulary, 11, 73, 161, 235, 315, 389, 465, 539, 601, 651, 703

Units of Measure. *See* Length

Units of measurement, *599E, 635, 639A*

Unknown numbers, 621

Unlock the Problem, 49, 135, 217, 285, 365, 421, 503, 565, 621, 683, 765

Use Diagrams, 726, 732, 768

Use Graphs, 661

Use Models, 470, 517

Use Reasoning, 22, 143, 213, 544

Value, *649E, 671B*

Venn diagrams, 102, 161

Vertex/Vertices, *701H,* 711–714, 723–726, *724*

Visual Boxing, *463H*

Visualize It, 11, 73, 161, 235, 315, 389, 465, 539, 601, 651, 703

Vocabulary

Chapter at a Glance, 9A–9D, 71A–71C, 159A–159D, 233A–233D, 313A–313D, 387A–387D, 463A–463D, 537A–537D, 599A–599D, 649A–649C, 701A–701D

Chapter Vocabulary, 9H, 71H, 159H, 233H, 313H, 387H, 463H, 537H, 599H, 649H, 701H

Chapter Vocabulary Cards, At the beginning of every chapter.

Developing Math Language, 9H, 71H, 159H, 233H, 313H, 387H, 463H, 537H, 599H, 649H, 701H

ELL Vocabulary Activity, 9H, 71H, 159H, 233H, 313H, 387H, 463H, 537H, 599H, 649H, 701H

Vocabulary Builder, 11, 73, *75B, 99B, 105B, 141B,* 161, *163B, 169B,* 235, *255B, 267B, 273B, 297B,* 315, *317B, 341B, 347B,* 389, *391B, 415B,* 465, *467B, 491B,* 539, *571B, 577B,* 601, *627B, 639B,* 651, *653B, 671B,* 703, *729B, 747B*

Vocabulary Preview, 11, 73, 161, 235, 315, 389, 465, 539, 601, 651, 703

Vocabulary Review, 11, 73, 157, 161, 235, 315, 389, 461, 465, 539, 601, 651, 703

Vocabulary Strategy

Graphic Organizers, 9H, 159H, 313H, 463H, 537H, 599H, 649H

Word Wall, 233H, 649H, 701H

Vocabulary Games, *12A–12D, 74A–74B, 162A–162D, 236A–236B, 316A–316B, 390A–390B, 466A–466D, 540A–540B, 602A–602B, 652A–652B, 704A–704D*

Vocabulary Story, 1–8, 150–151–158, 455–462, 693–700

Weeks, *538A*

Whole Group Options, *9F, 71F, 159F, 233F, 313F, 387F, 463F, 537F, 599F, 649F, 701F*

Whole-part relationship. *See* Part-whole relationship

Why Teach This, *25A, 31A, 49A, 87A, 99A, 163A, 169A, 181A, 237A, 255A, 279A, 291A, 341A, 365A, 371A, 479A, 521A, 547A, 565A, 577A, 609A, 639A, 653A, 659A, 697A, 729A, 741A*

Word form of numbers, 37–39, *105A*, 105–108, 111–113

Word of the Day. *See Problem of the Day*

Word problems, *translating into number sentences, 291A, 371A. See also Problem Types, for word problems*

Word Wall, *233H, 649H, 701H*

Write Math, 16, 22, 28, 34, 46, 58, 64, 78, 84, 90, 96, 108, 120, 132, 144, 157, 166, 172, 178, 184, 190, 202, 208, 214, 220, 226, 240, 246, 252, 258, 264, 270, 275, 282, 288, 294, 300, 306, 320, 326, 332, 338, 356, 362, 374, 380, 394, 400, 406, 412, 424, 430, 436, 442, 448, 470, 476, 482, 488, 500, 506, 512, 518, 524, 530, 544, 550, 556, 562, 574, 580, 586, 592, 606, 612, 618, 630, 636, 642, 656, 662, 674, 680, 686, 708, 714, 726, 732, 738, 756, 762, 768

Writing

Math Journal, 16, 22, 28, 34, 39, 46, 52, 58, 64, 78, 84, 90, 96, 102, 108, 120, 126, 132, 138, 144, 166, 172, 178, 184, 190, 195, 202, 208, 214, 220, 226, 240, 246, 252, 258, 264, 270, 275, 282, 288, 294, 300, 306, 320, 326, 332, 338, 344, 349, 356, 362, 368, 374, 380, 394, 400, 406, 412, 417, 424, 430, 436, 442, 448, 470, 476, 482, 488, 493, 506, 512, 518, 524, 530, 544, 550, 556, 562, 567, 574, 580, 586, 592, 606, 612, 618, 623, 630, 636, 642, 656, 662, 667, 674, 680, 686, 708, 714, 726, 732, 738, 743, 750, 756, 762, 768

story problems, 291A, 371A

Yardstick, 583–586

Zero, subtraction of, *348*, 445–448